Public Art in Lincoln Heights

As noticed by Ginger Mayerson

Public Art in Lincoln Heights, ISBN 978-1-942007-05-0 is published by The Wapshott Press, PO Box 31513, Los Angeles, California, 90031-0513, telephone 323-201-7147. All correspondence can be sent The Wapshott Press, PO Box 31513, LA CA 90031-0513. This collection is copyright © 2016 by The Wapshott Press, Los Angeles, California. Copyright © 2016 Ginger Mayerson and is reprinted here with the copyright owner's permission.

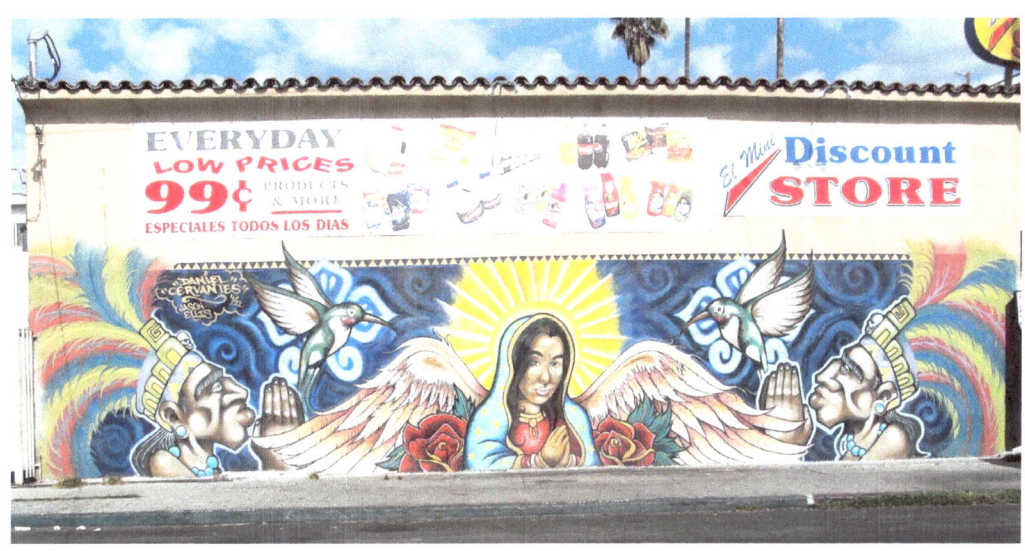

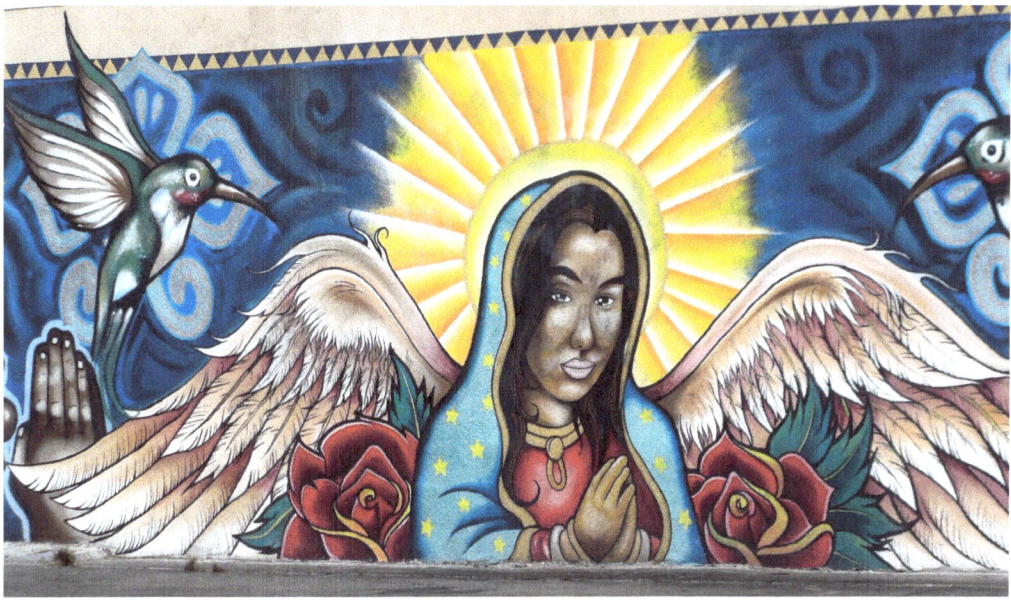

Ave 28 and Pasadena

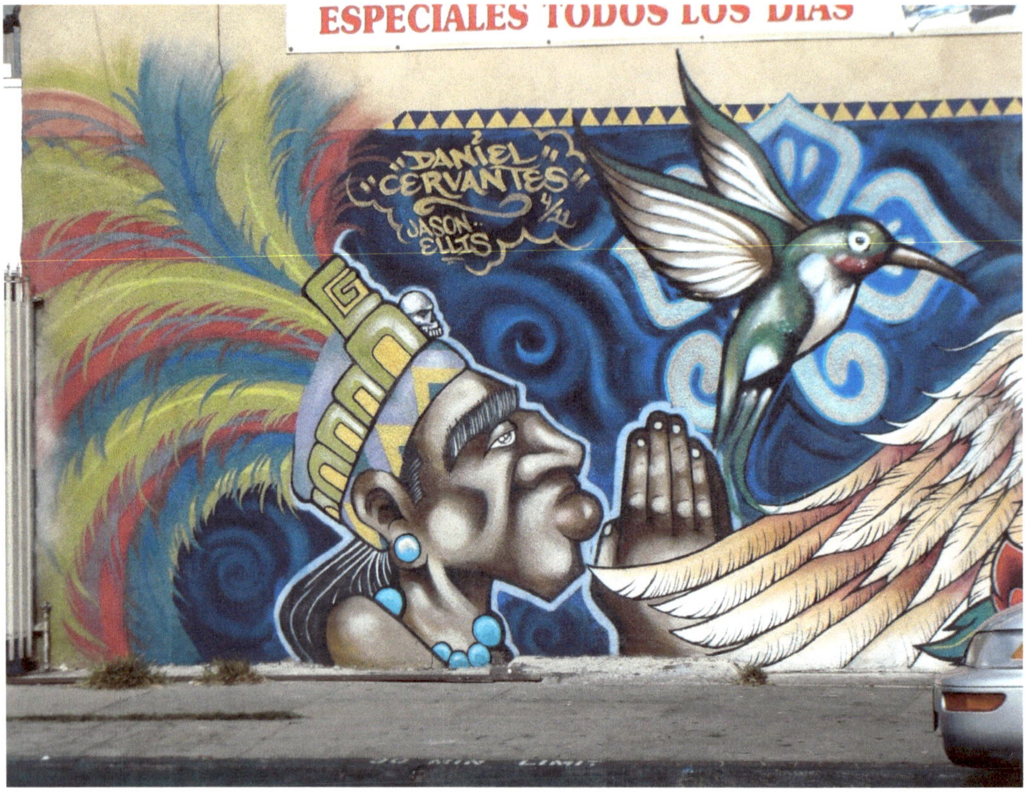

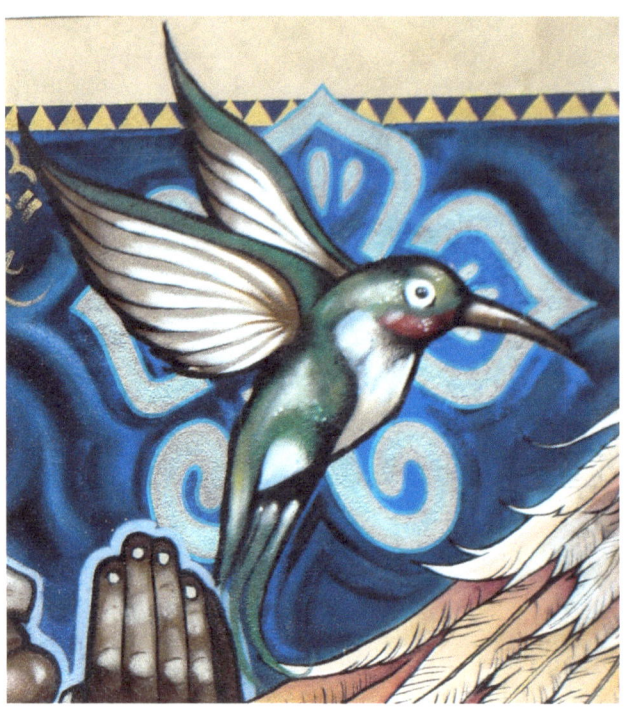

Ave 28 and Pasadena

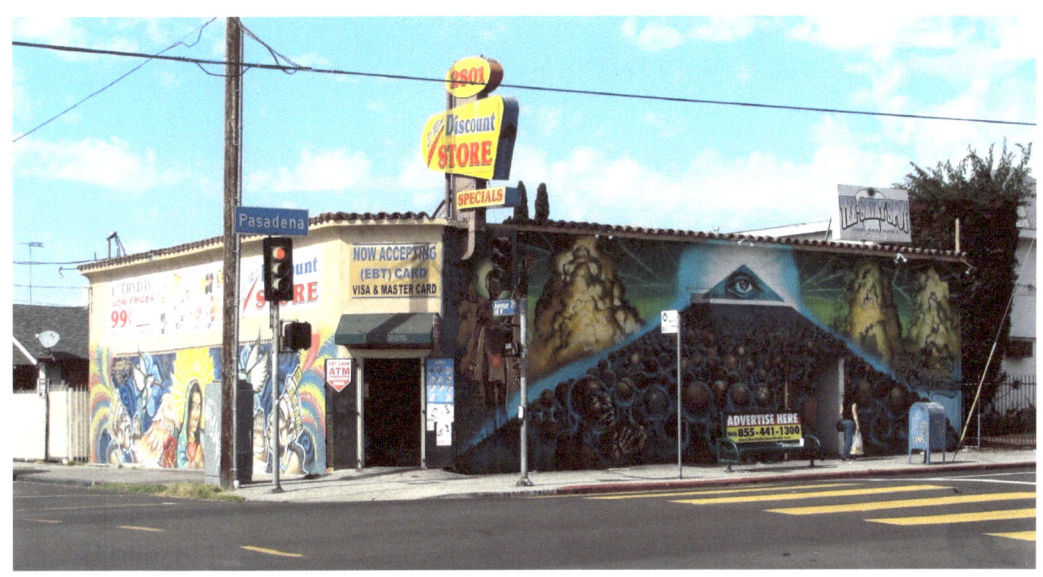

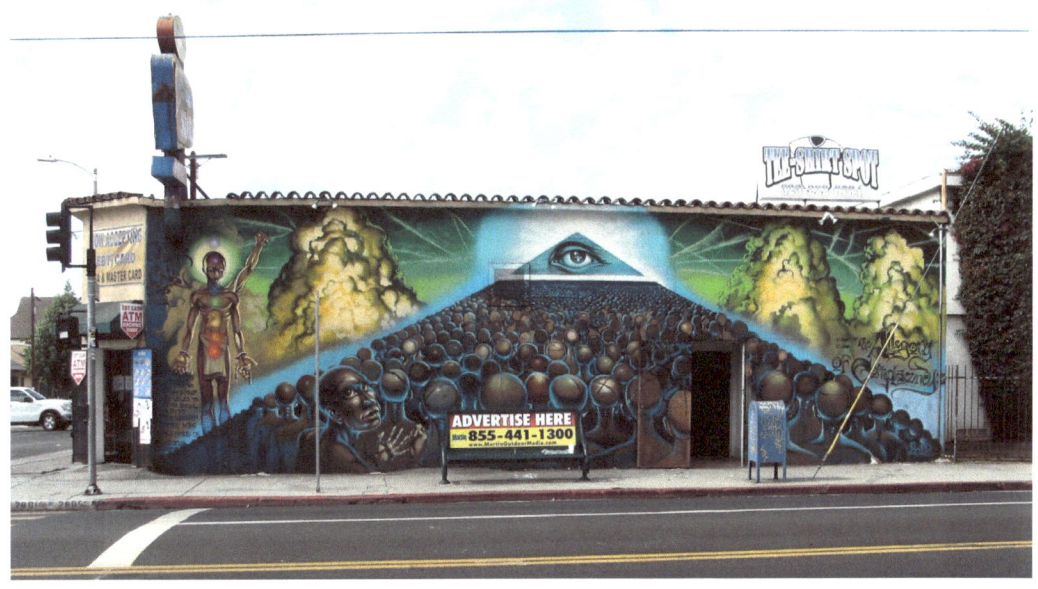

Ave 28 and Pasadena 2015

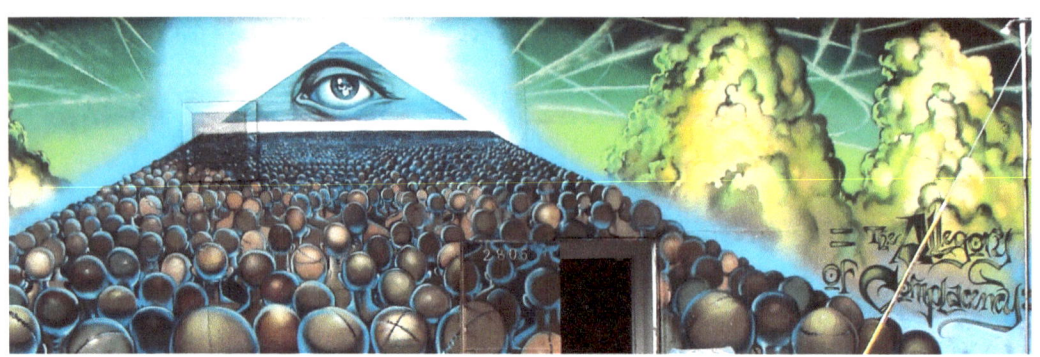

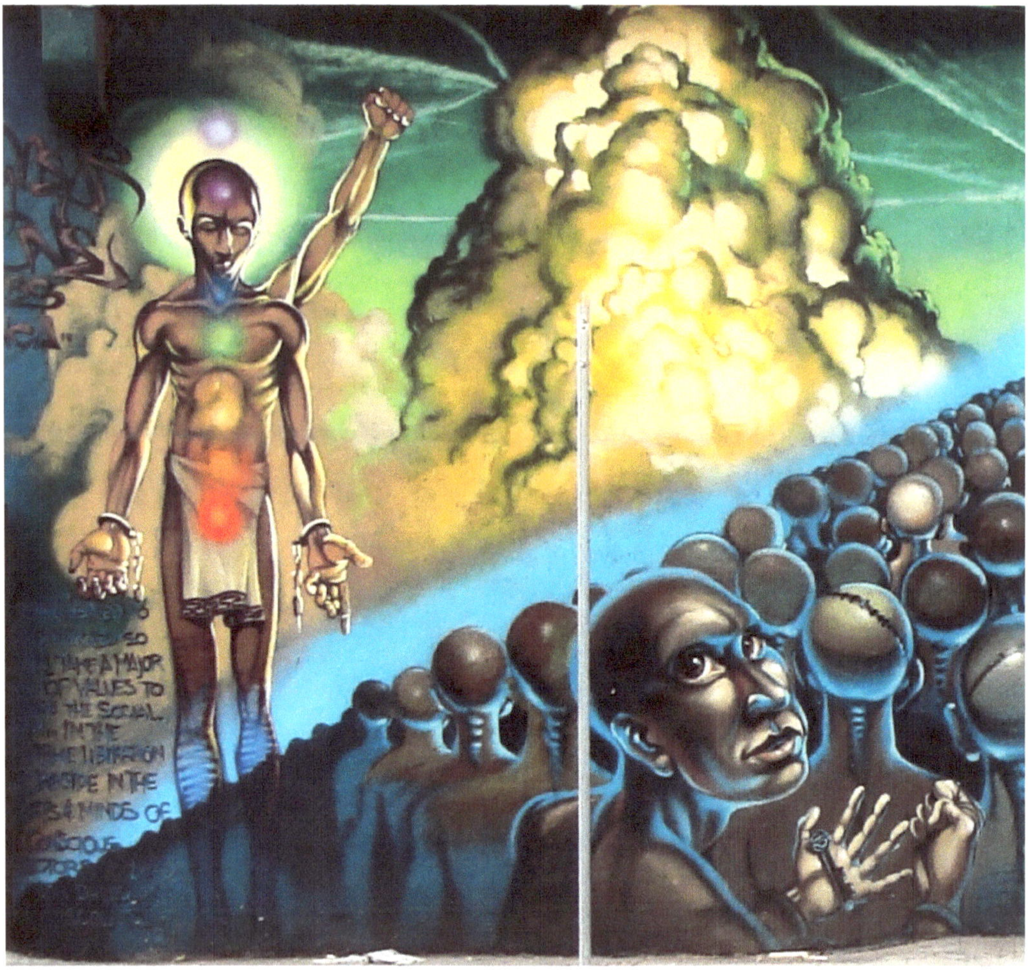

Ave 28 and Pasadena 2015

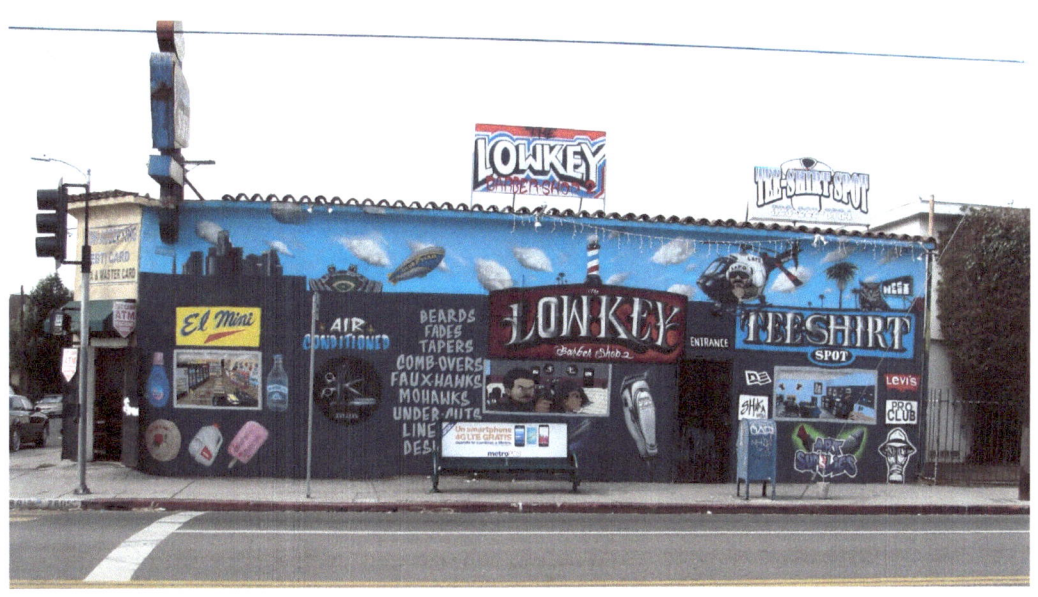

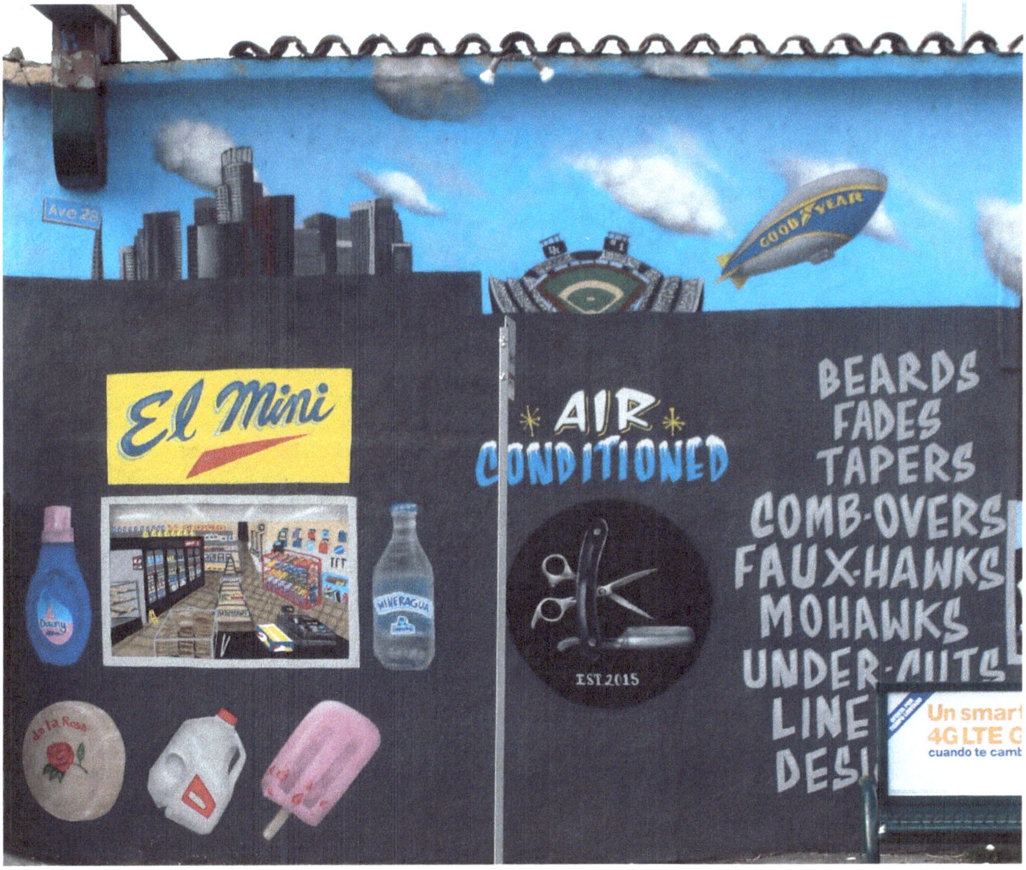

Ave 28 and Pasadena 2016

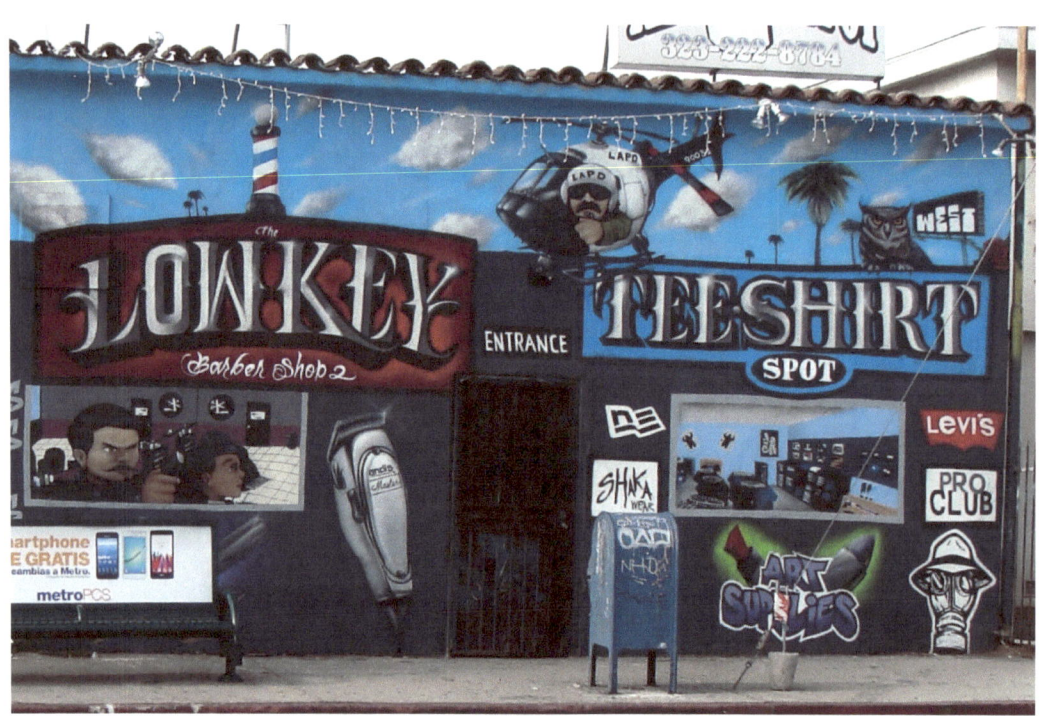

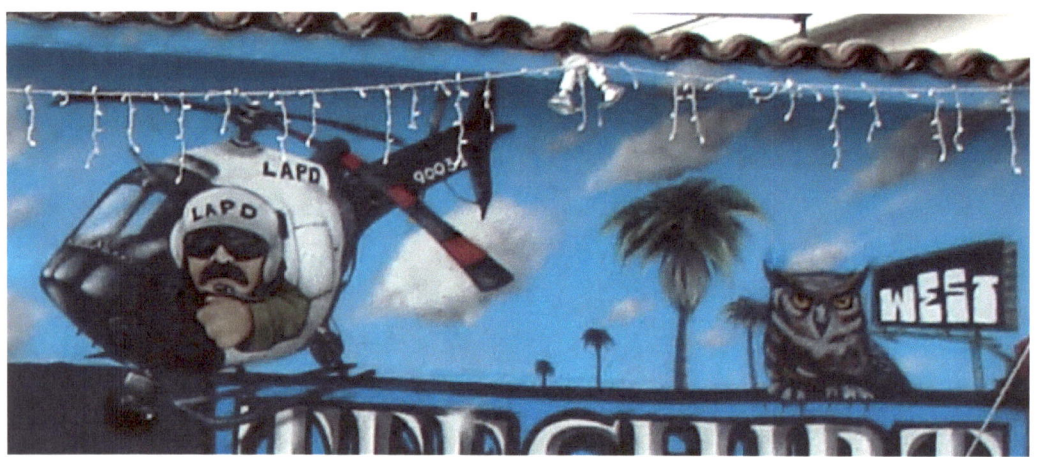

Ave 28 and Pasadena 2016

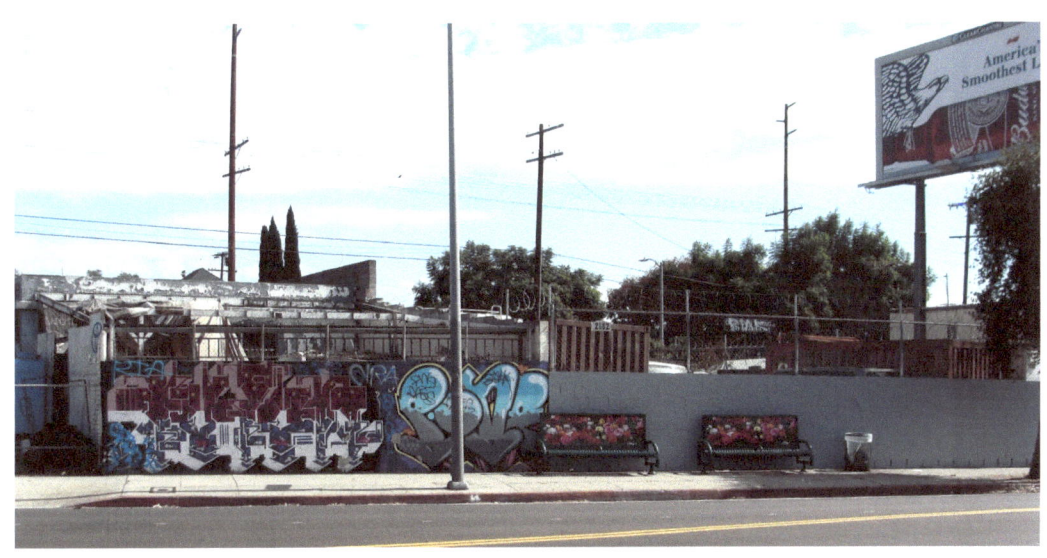
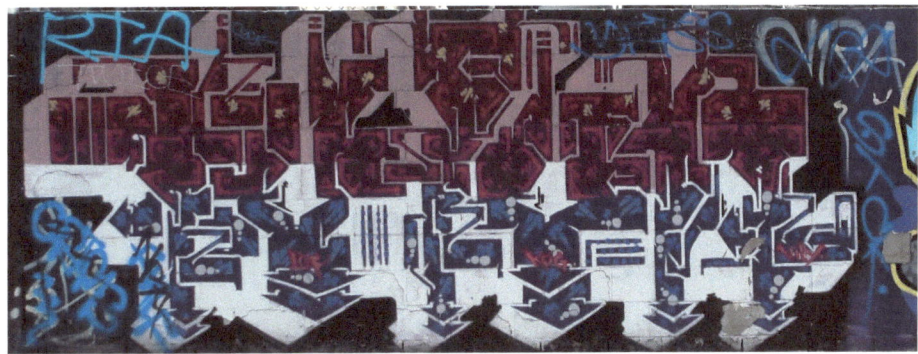
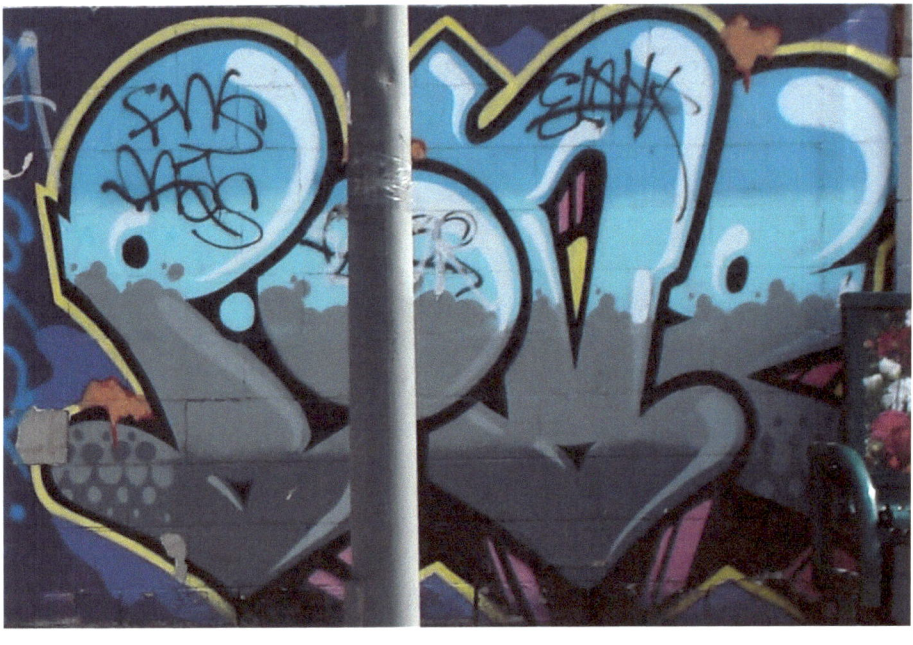

Ave 28 and Pasadena 2015

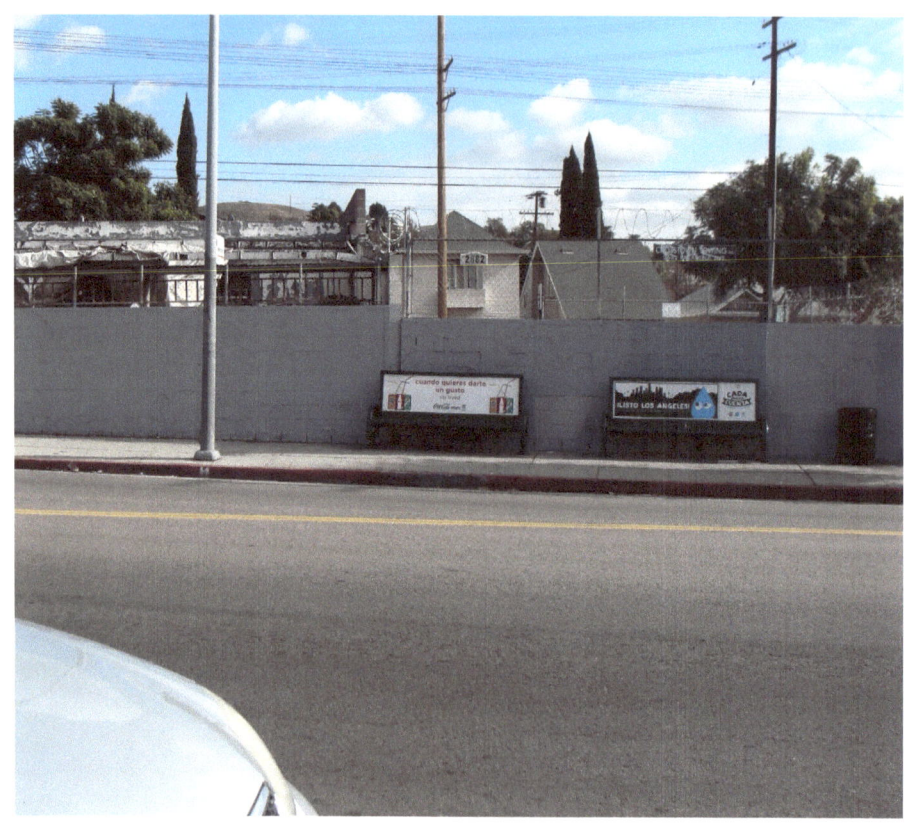
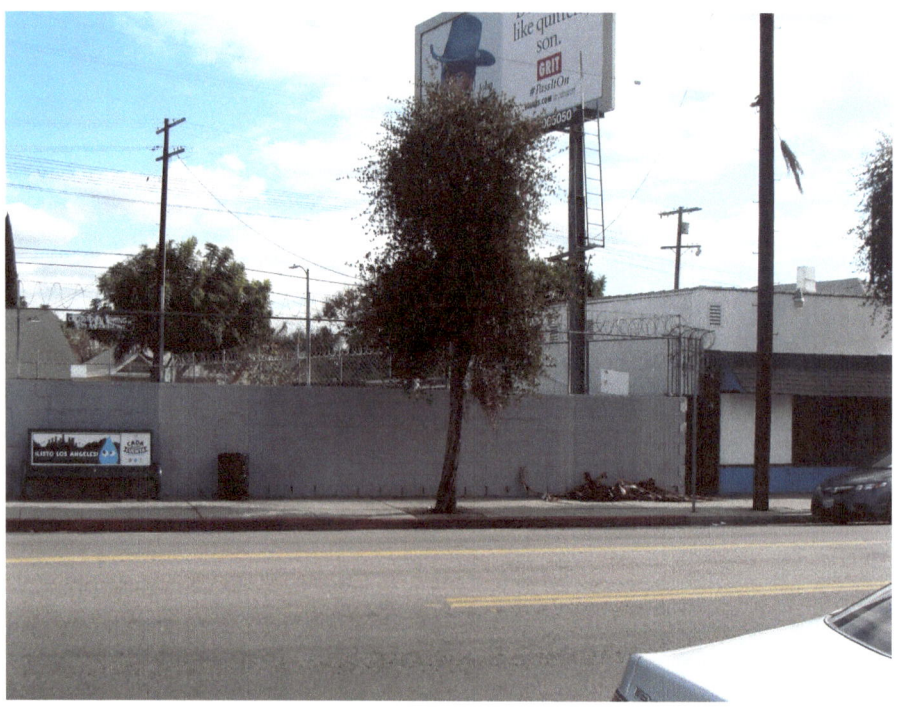

Ave 28 and Pasadena 2016

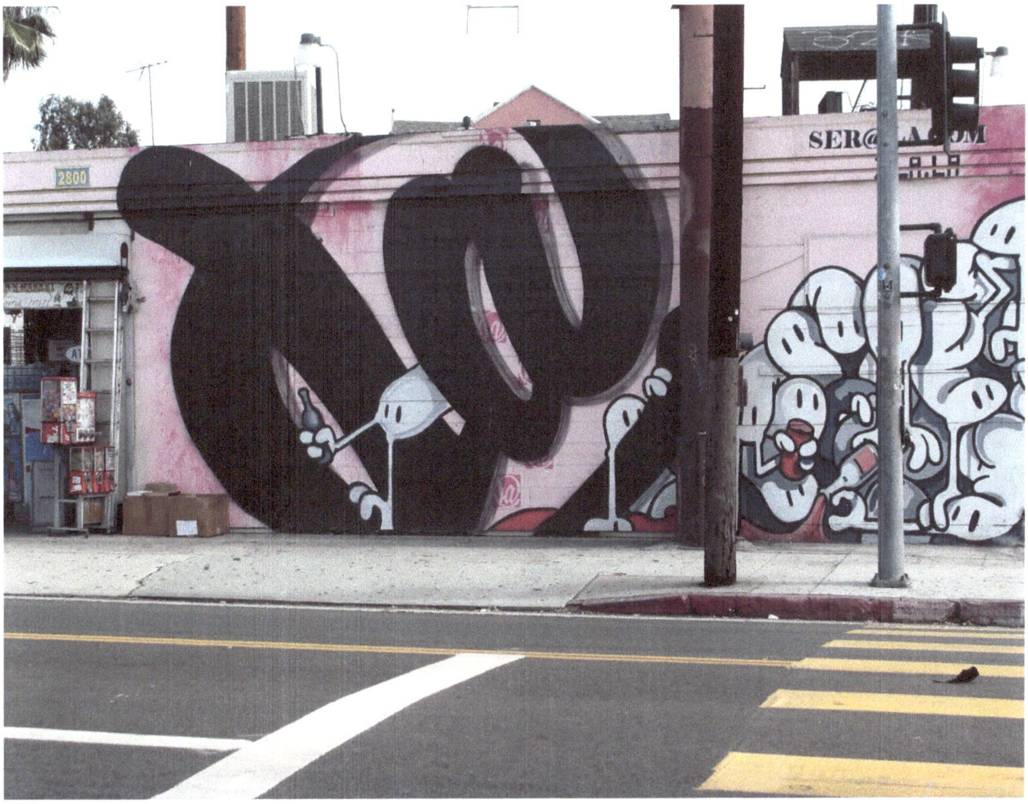

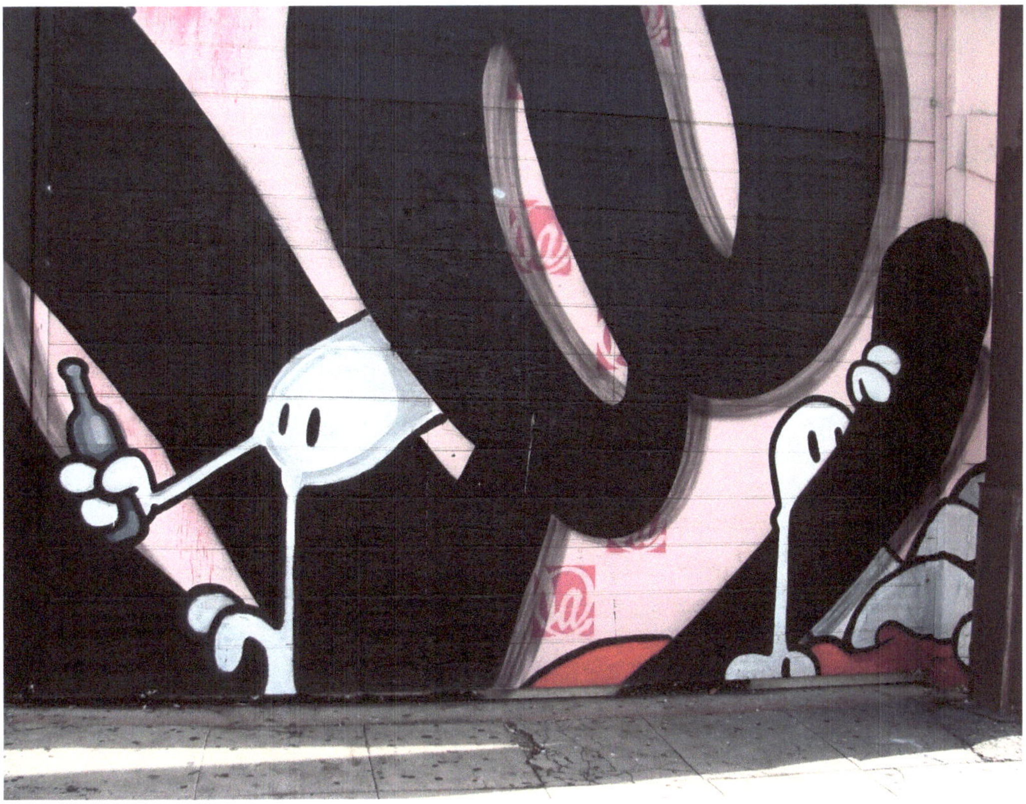

Ave 28 and Pasadena

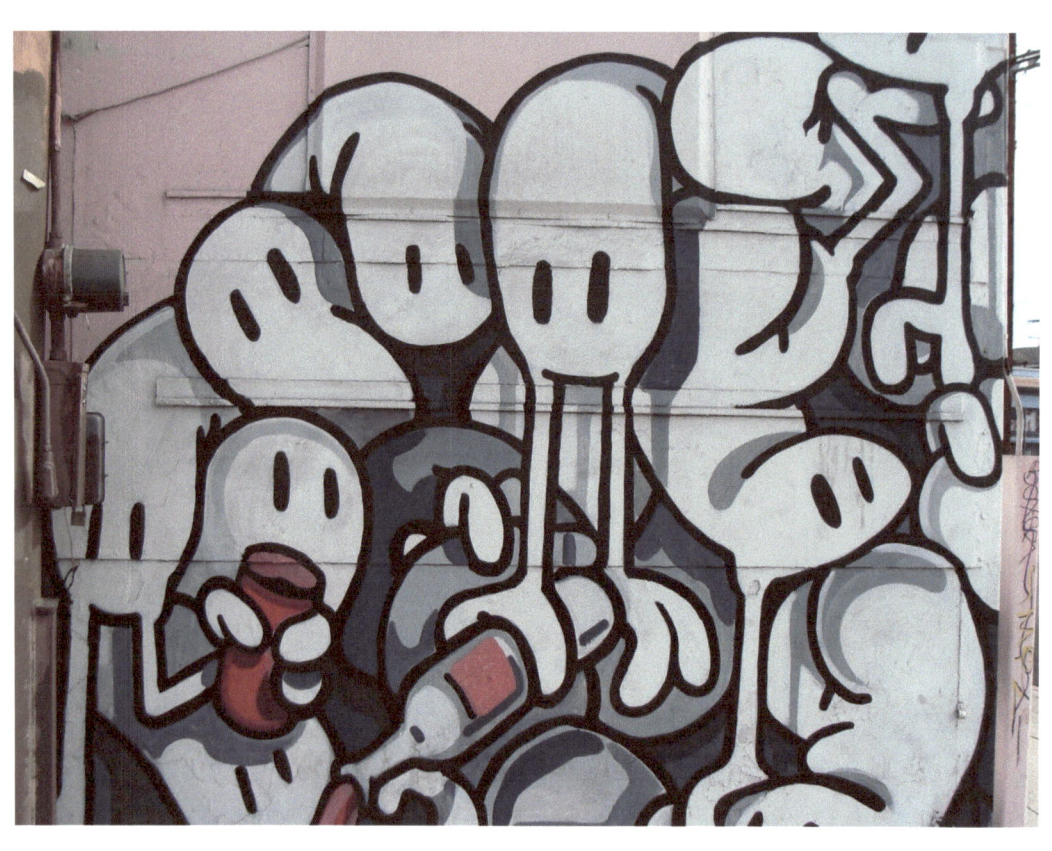

Ave 28 and Pasadena 2016

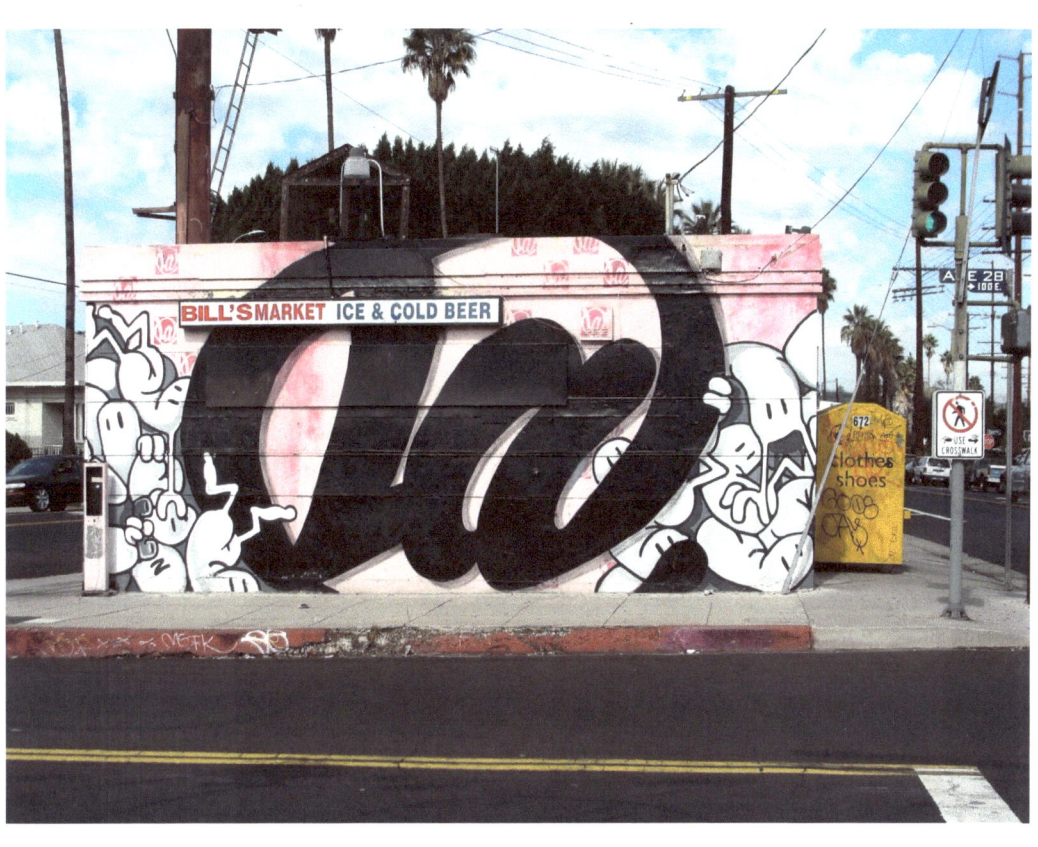

Ave 28 between Pasadena and Workman

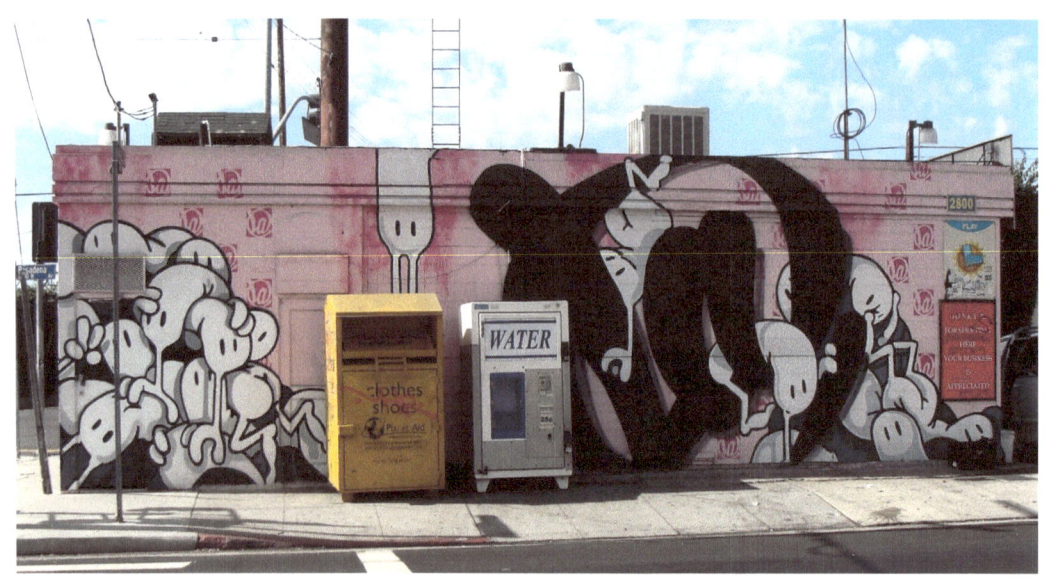

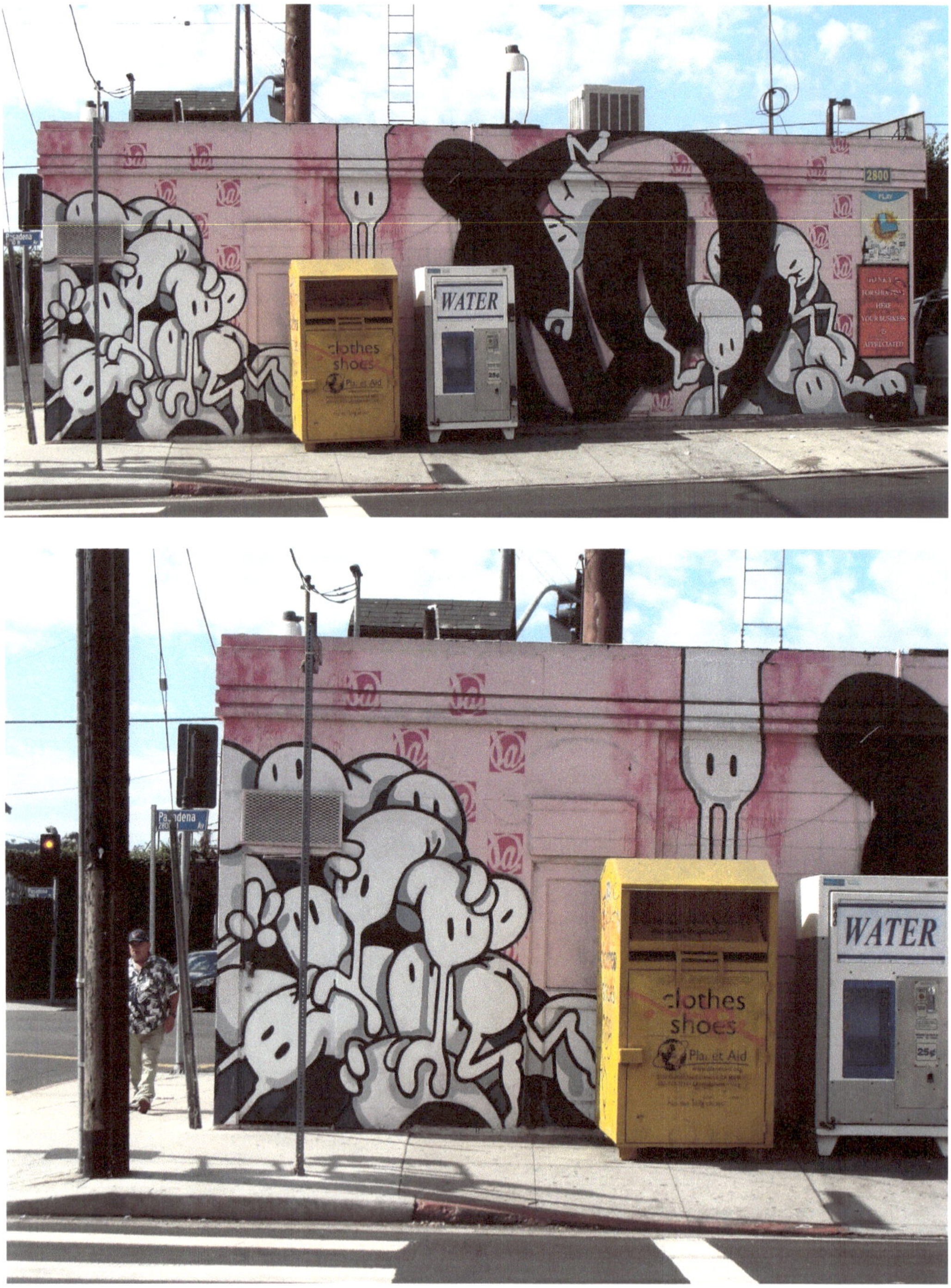

Ave 28 and Workman

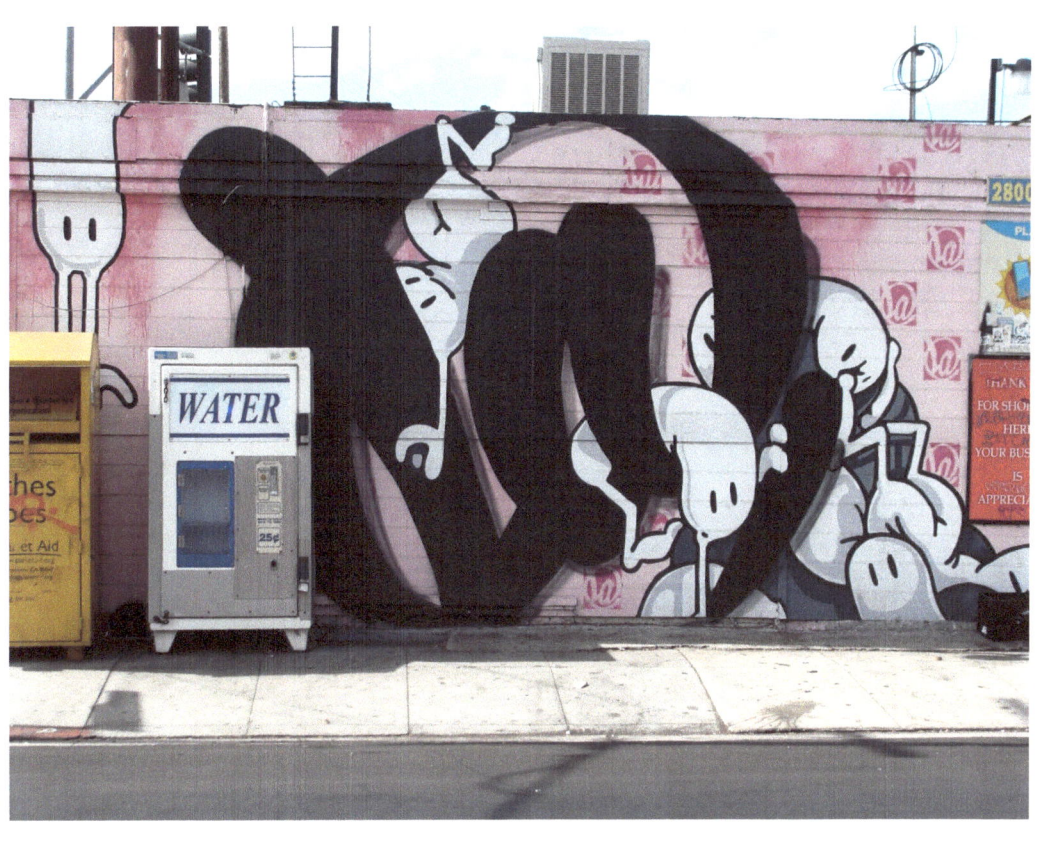

Ave 28 and Workman

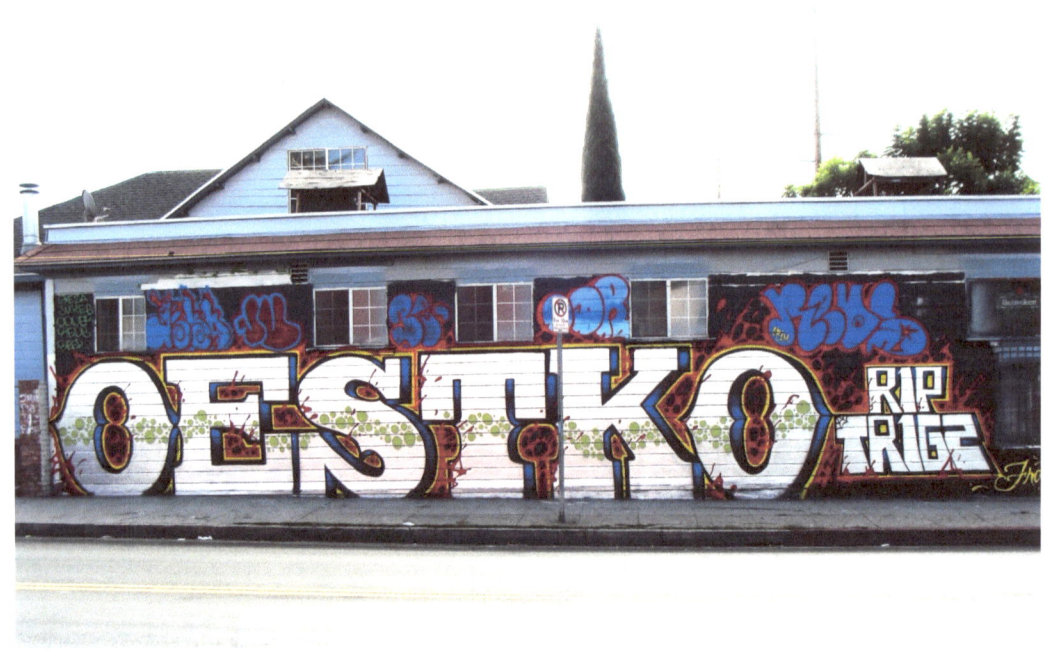

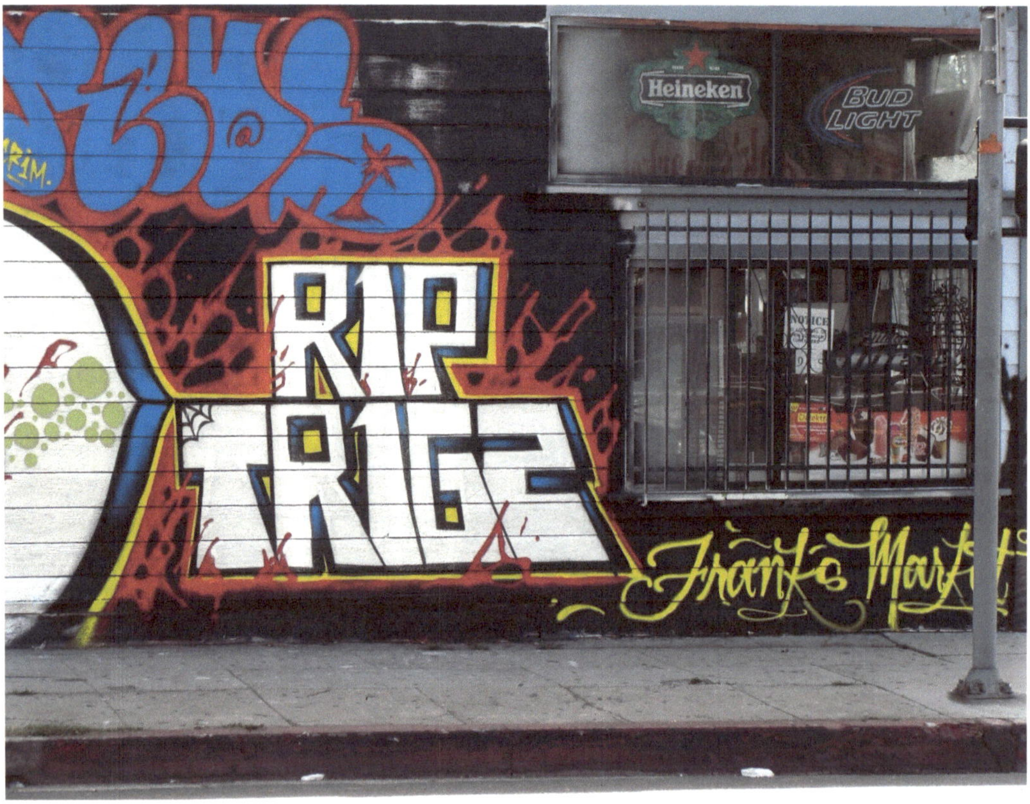

Ave 28 and Workman

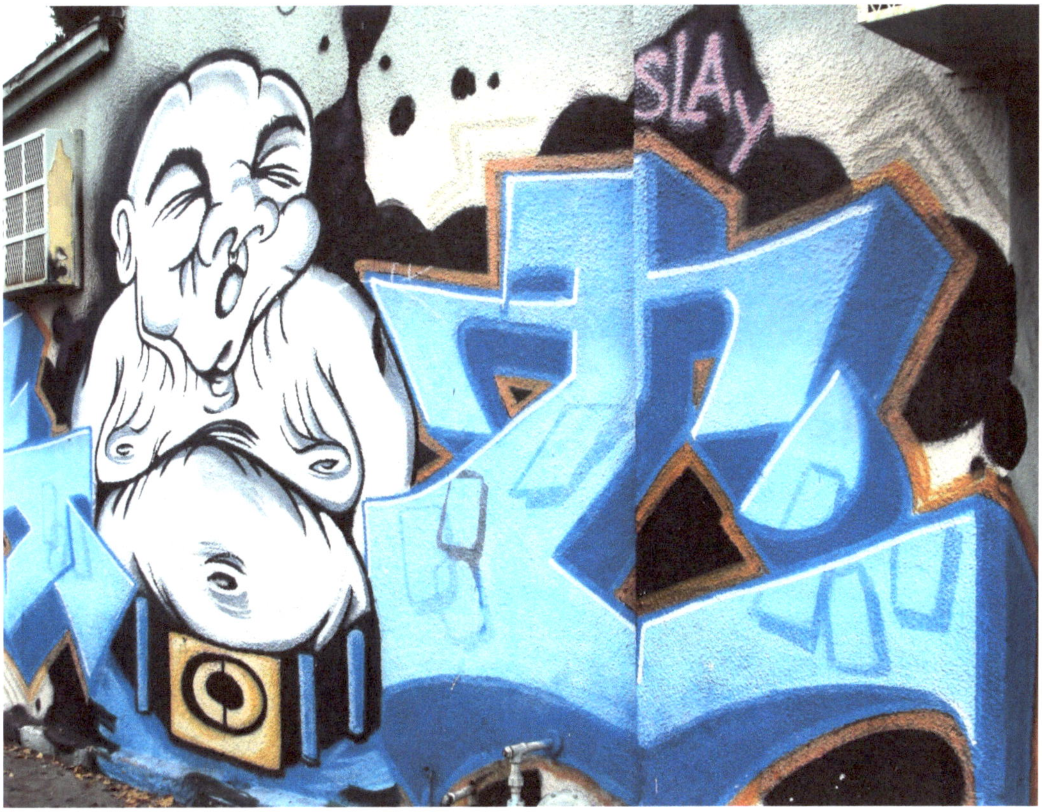

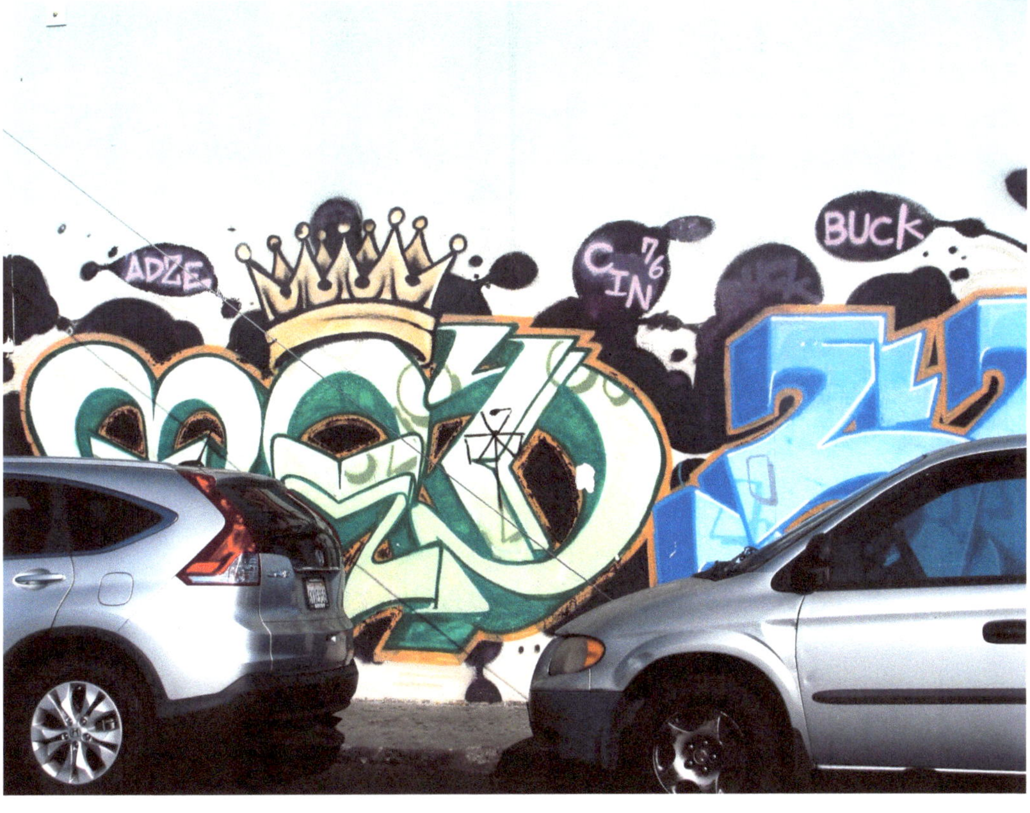

Ave 25 and 26

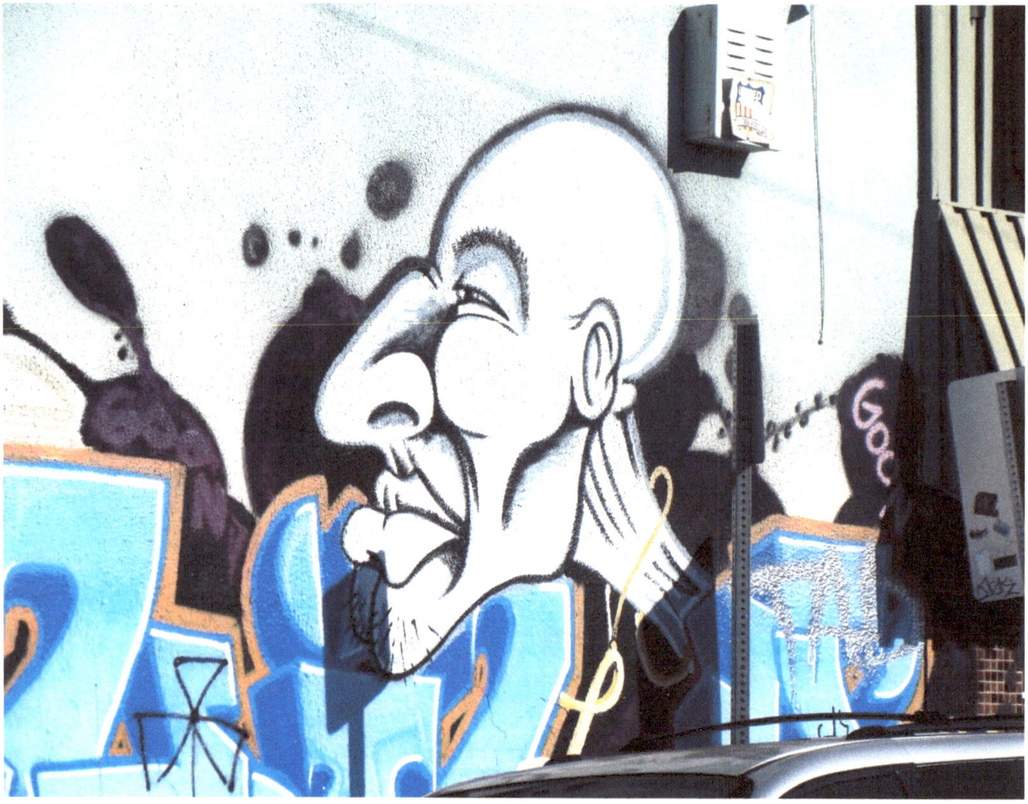

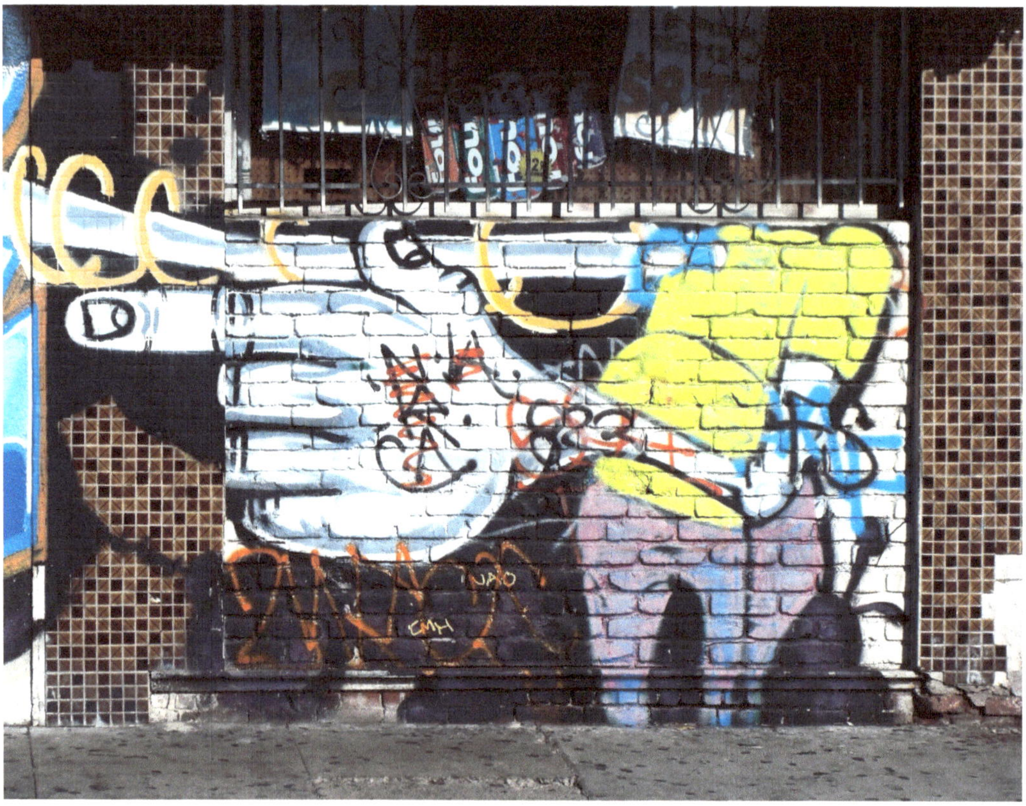

Ave 25 and 26

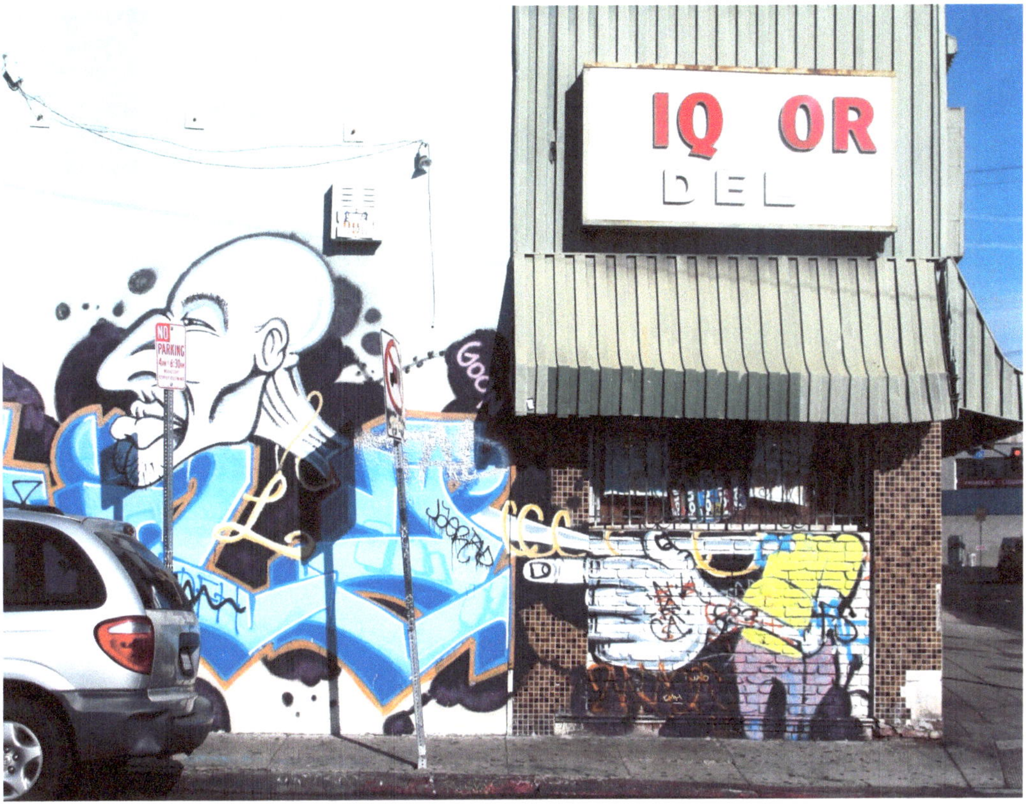

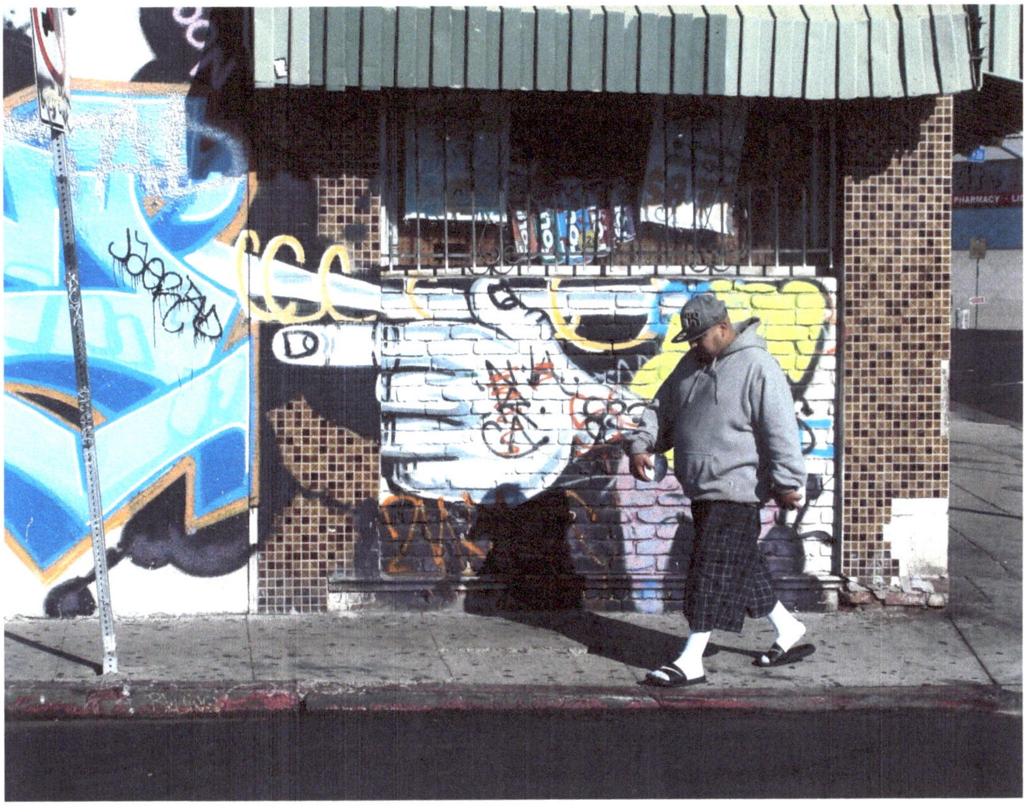

Ave 25 and 26

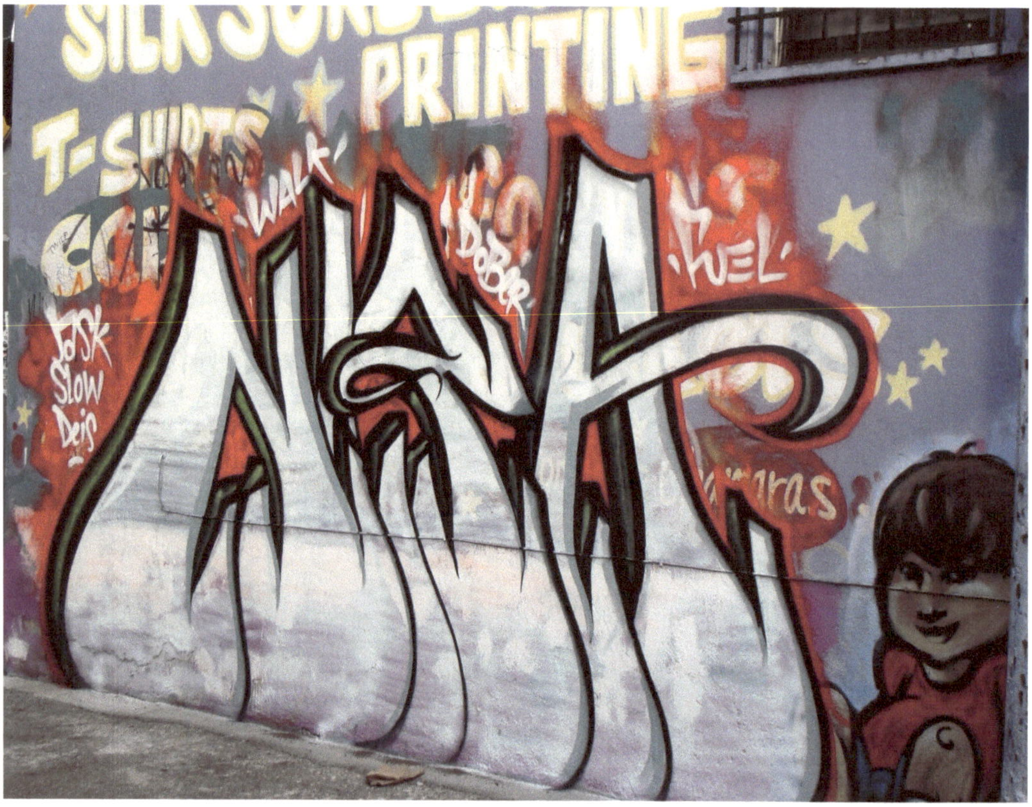

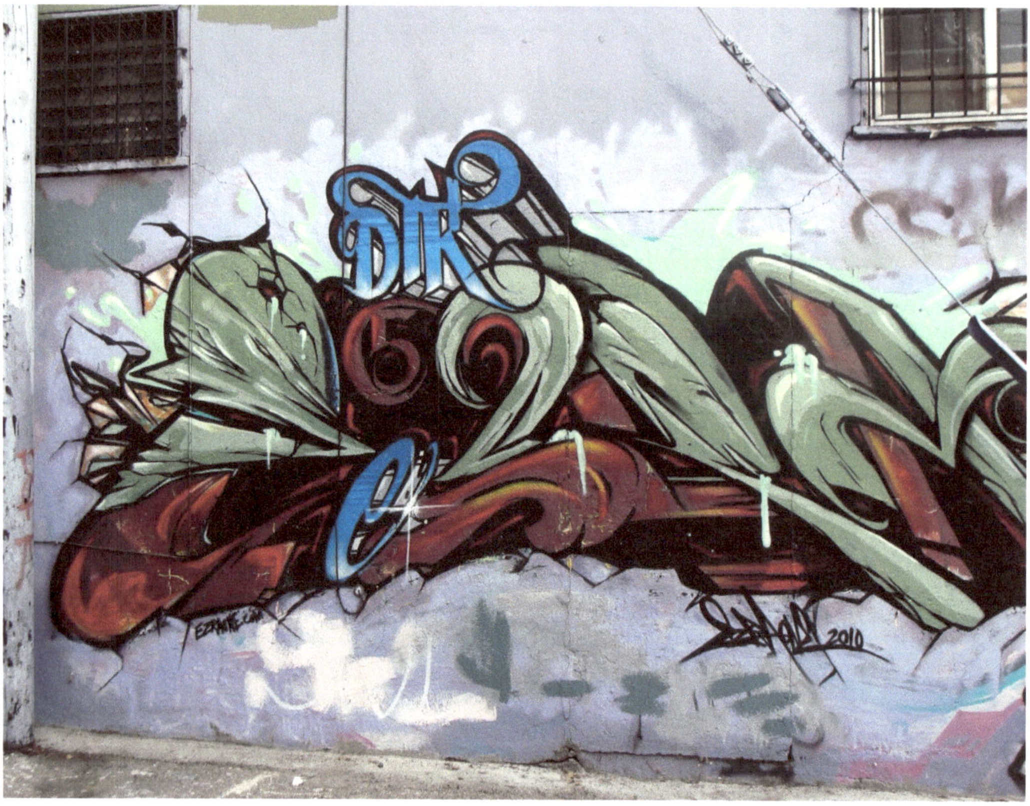

Alley off Daly 2015

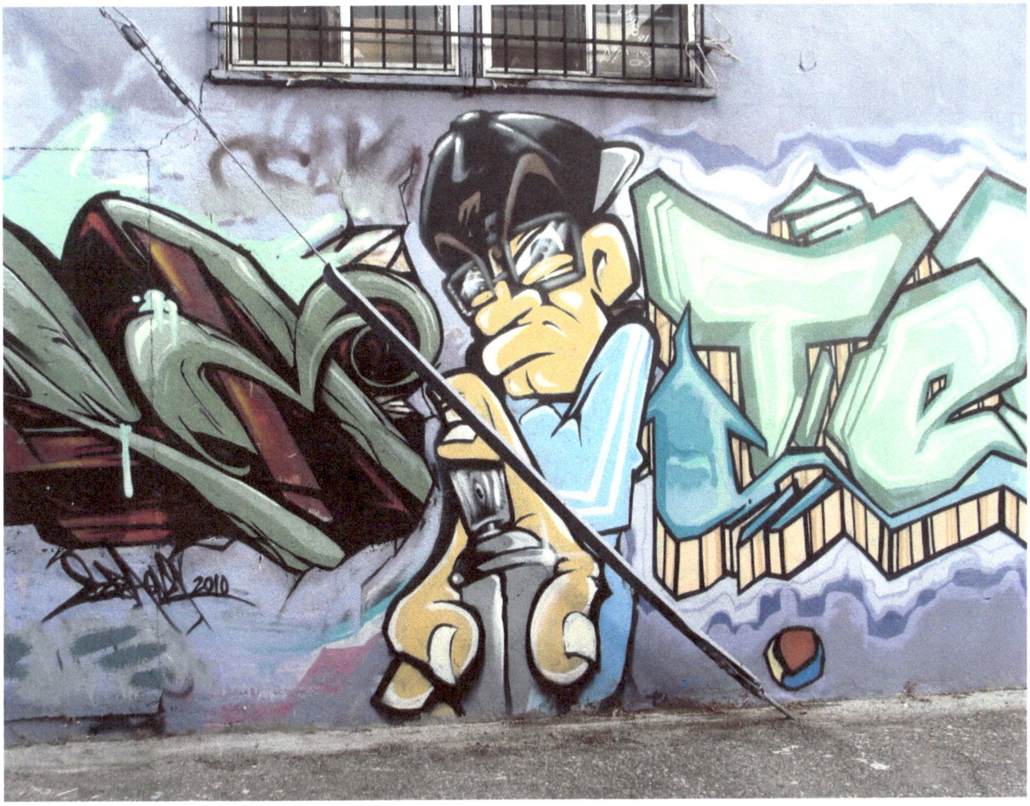

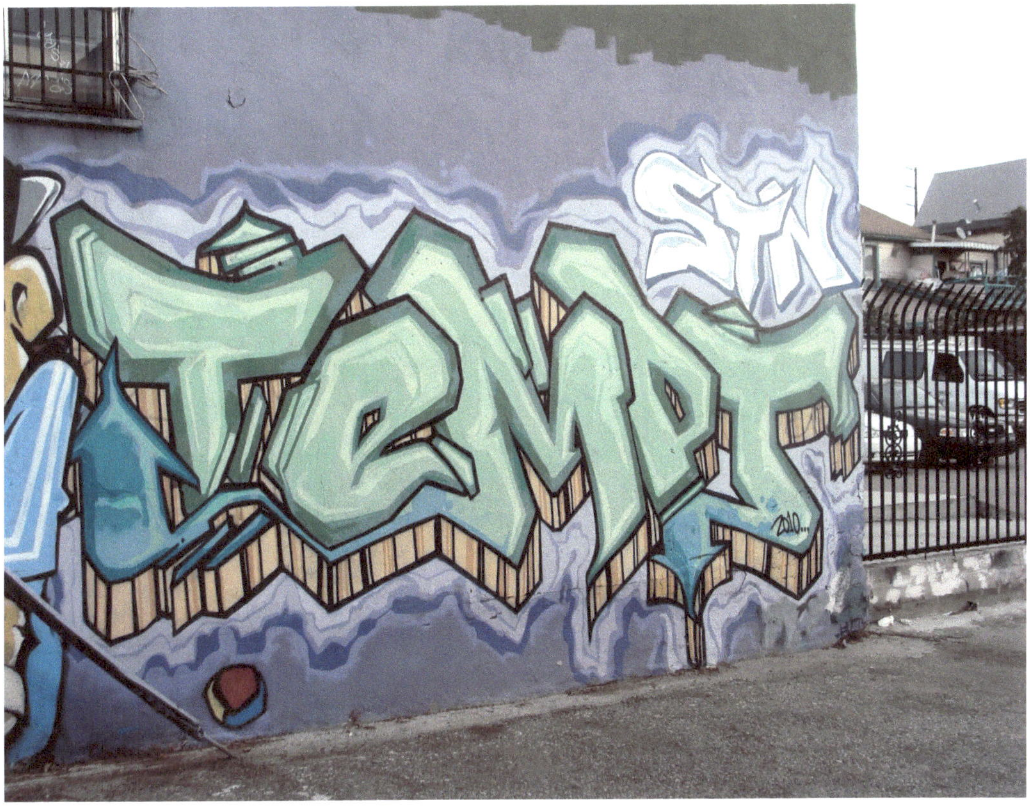

Alley off Daly 2015

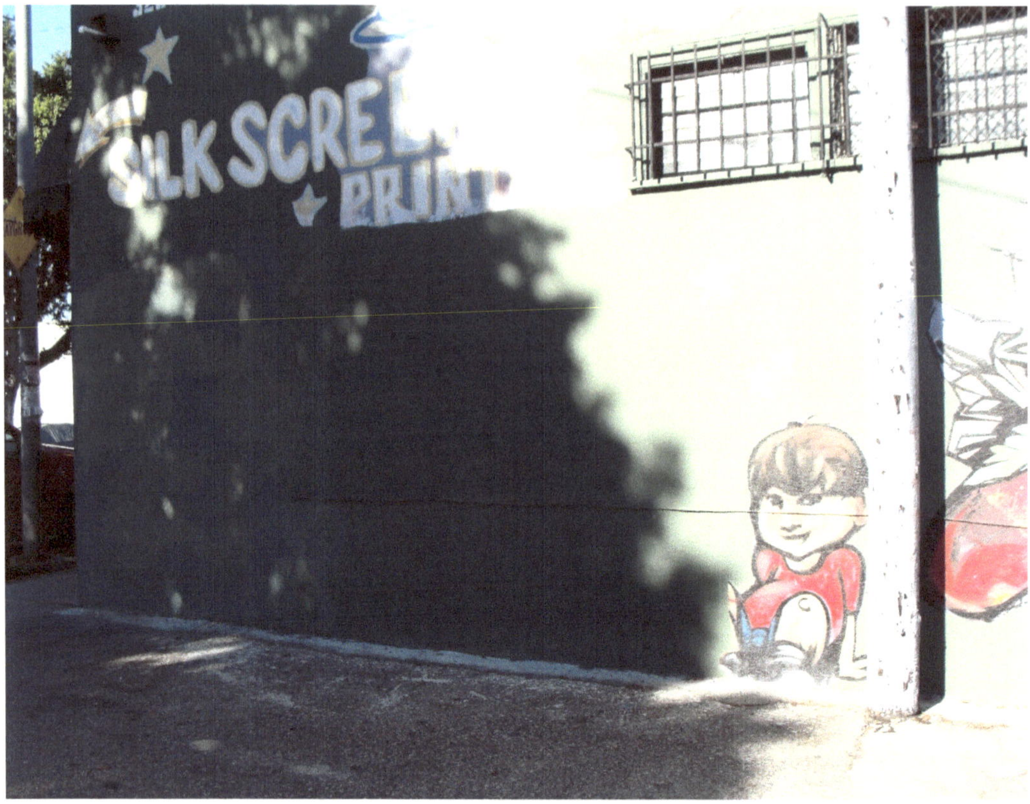

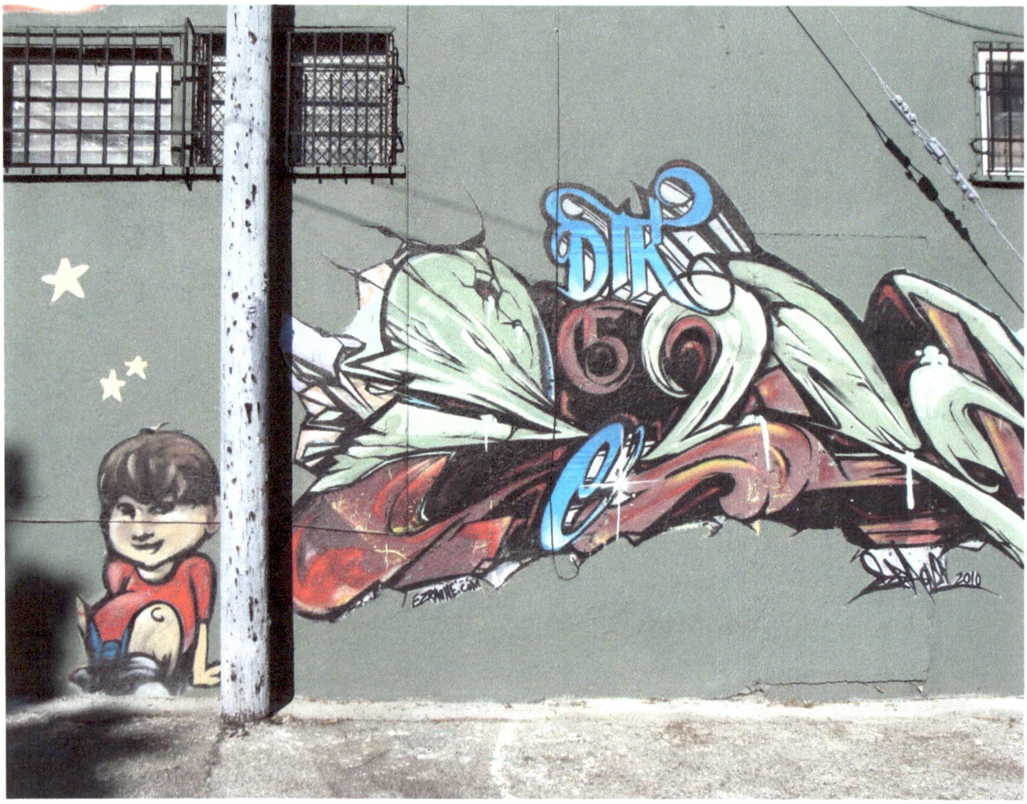

Alley off Daly 2016

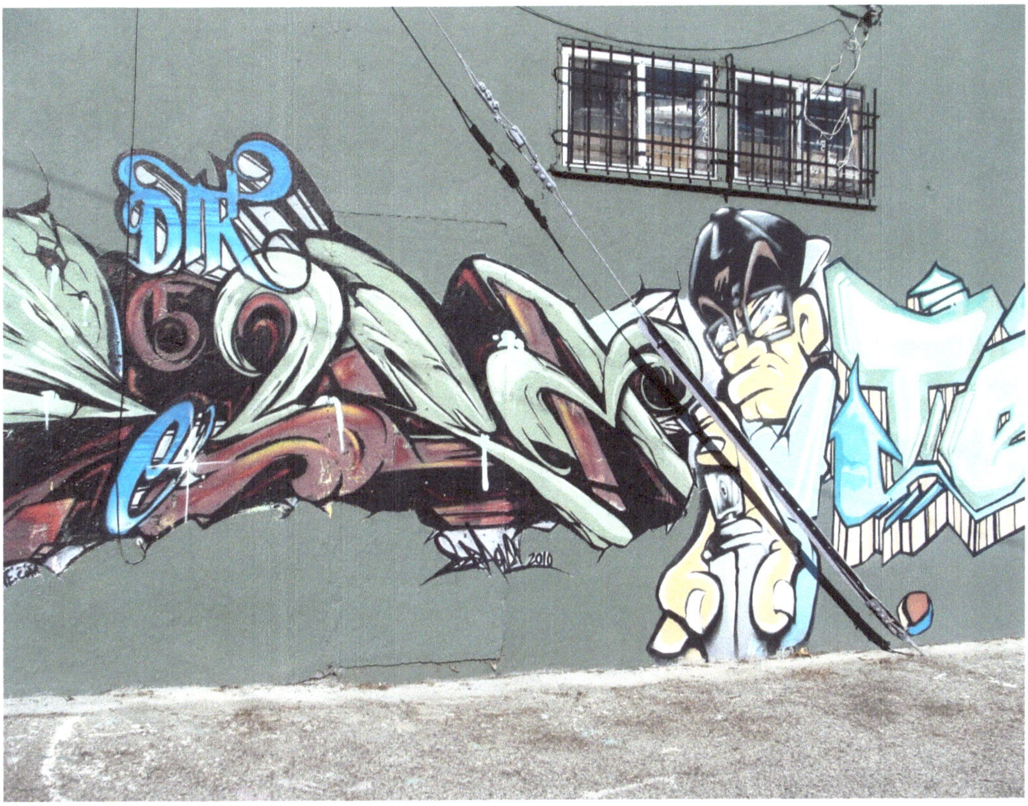

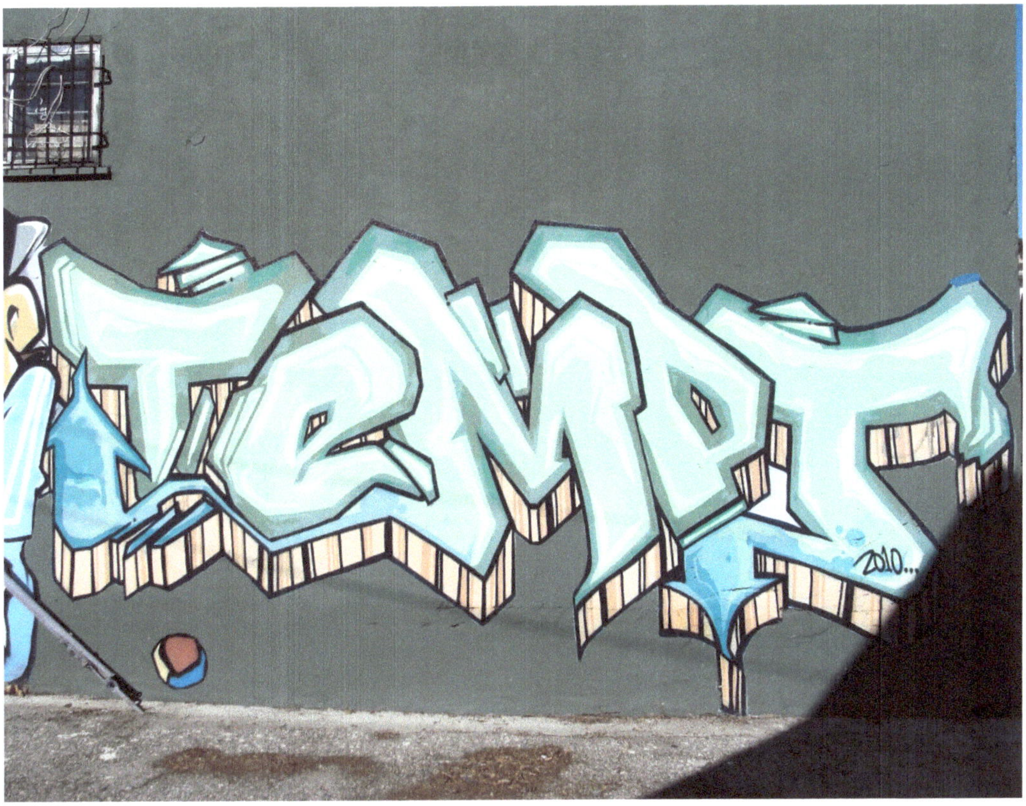

Alley off Daly 2016

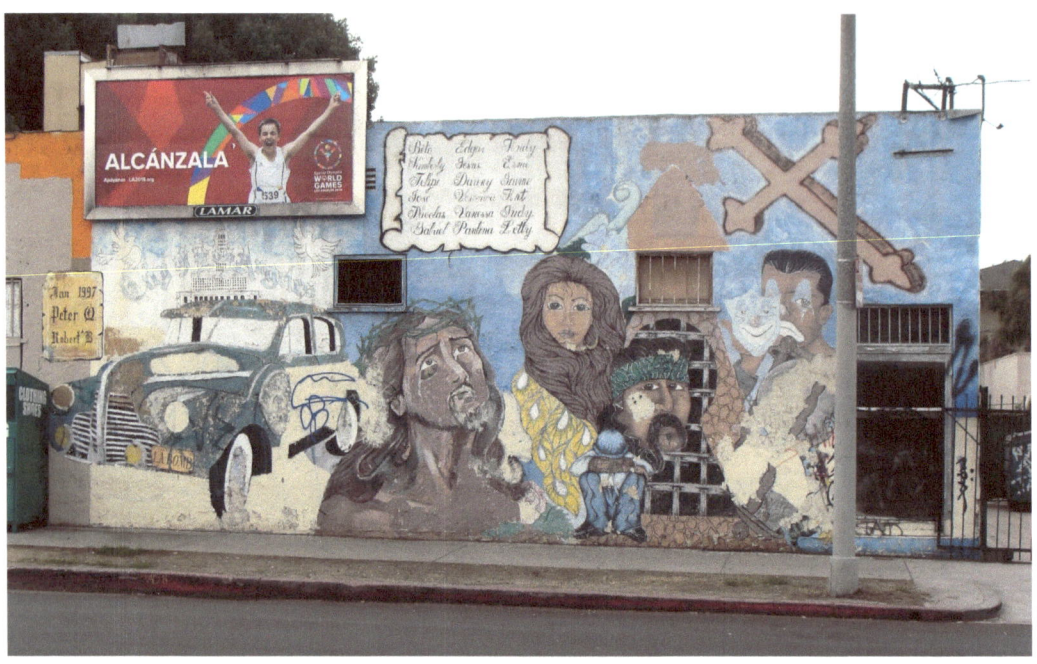

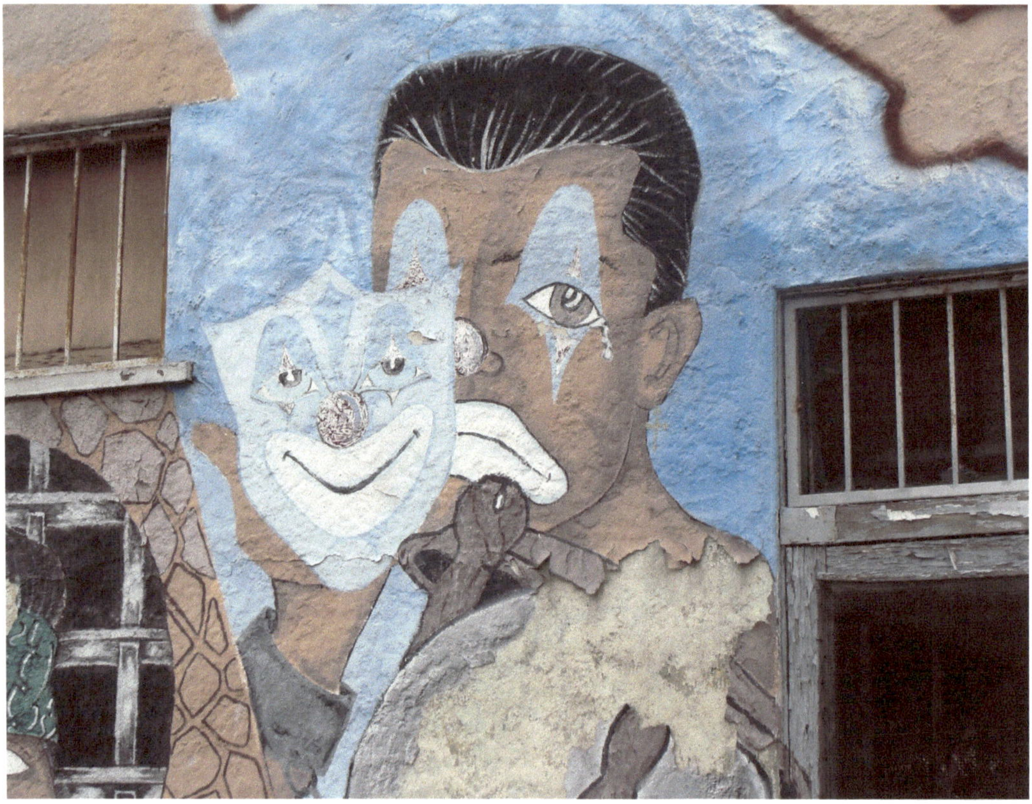

Manitou and Daly

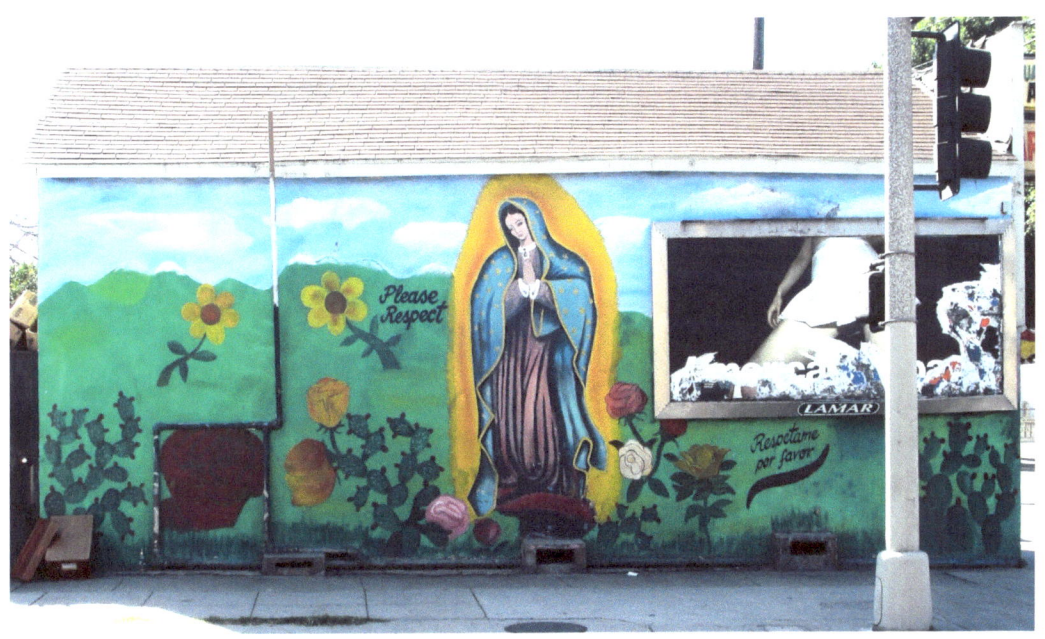

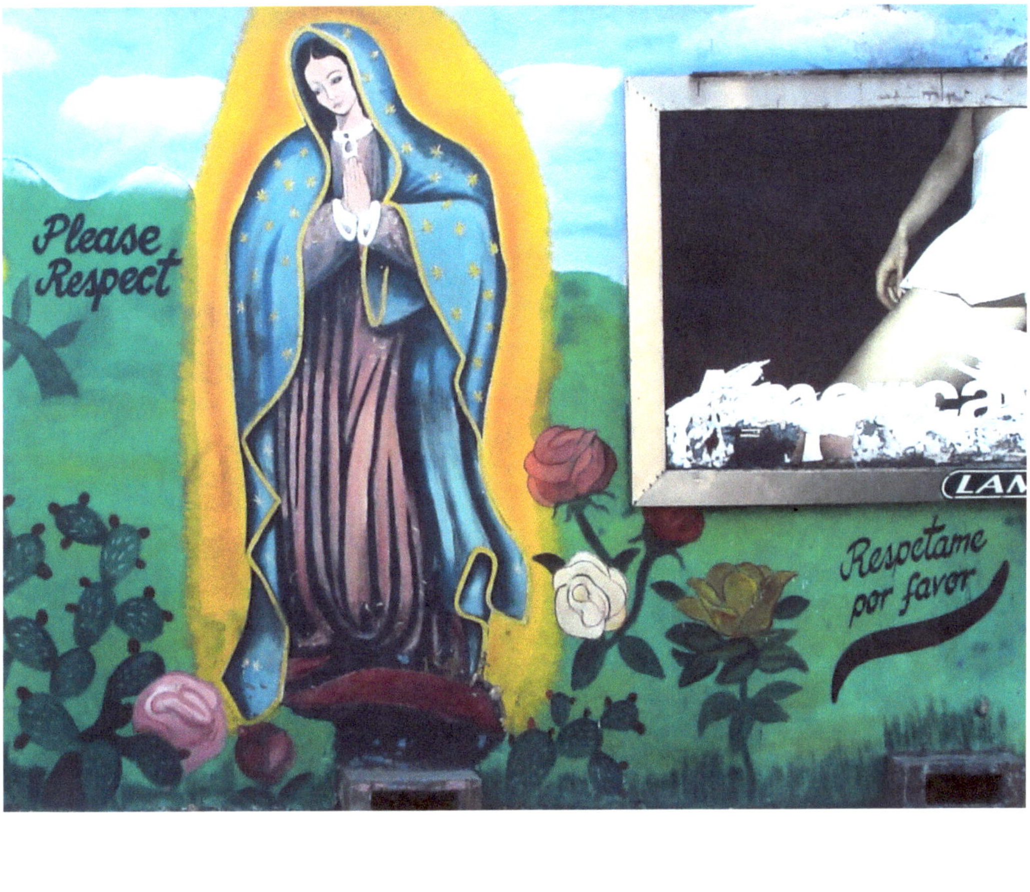

Mozart and Daly

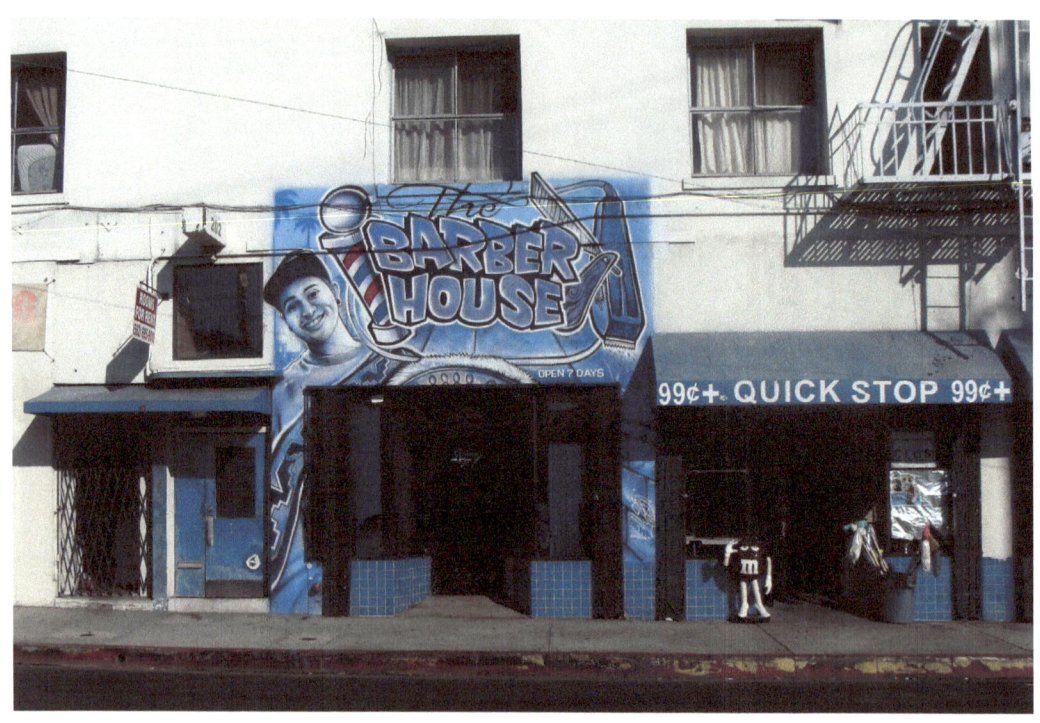

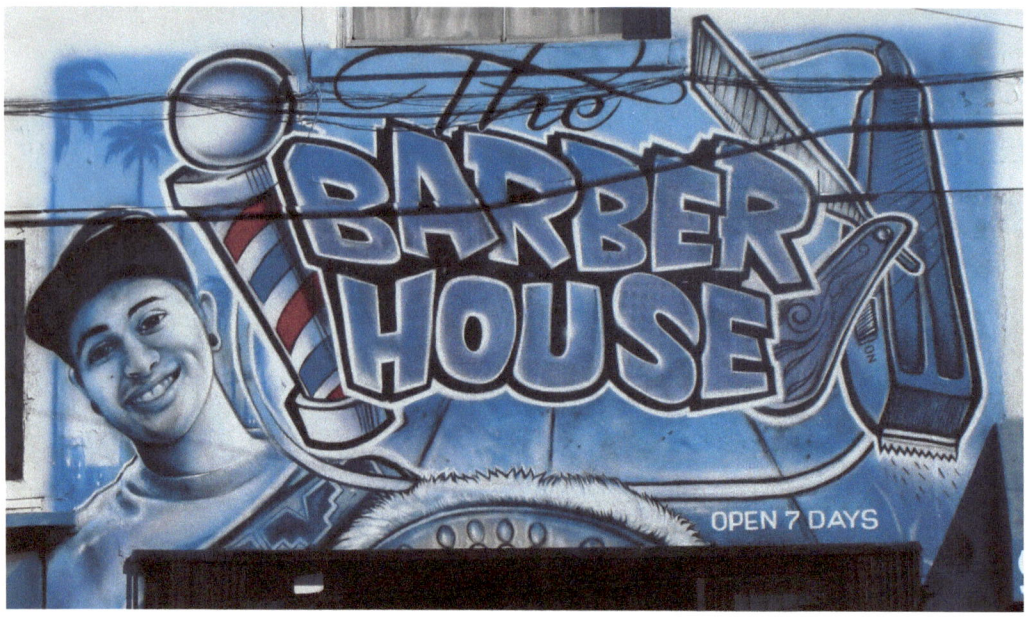

N Broadway and San Fernando

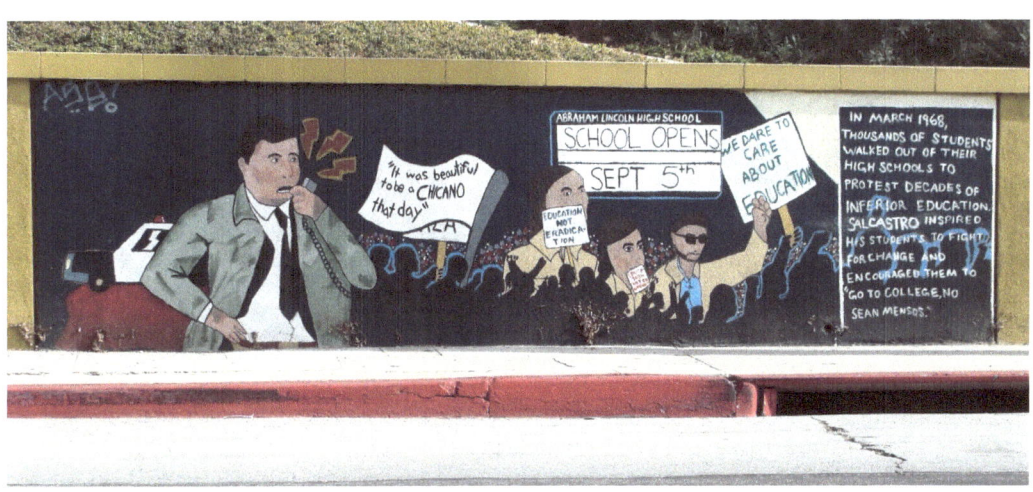
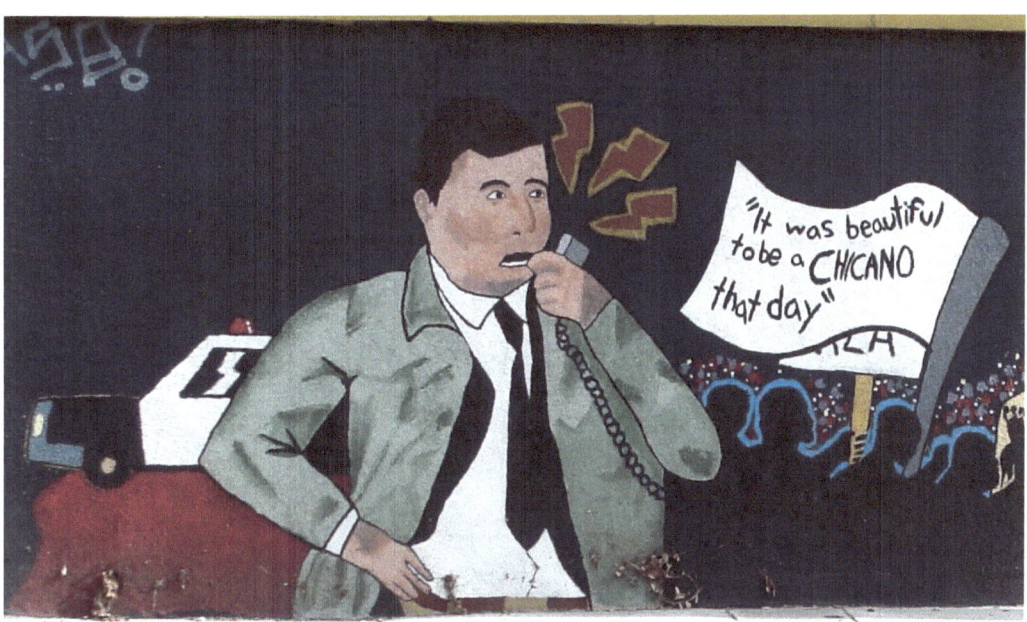

Lincoln High School

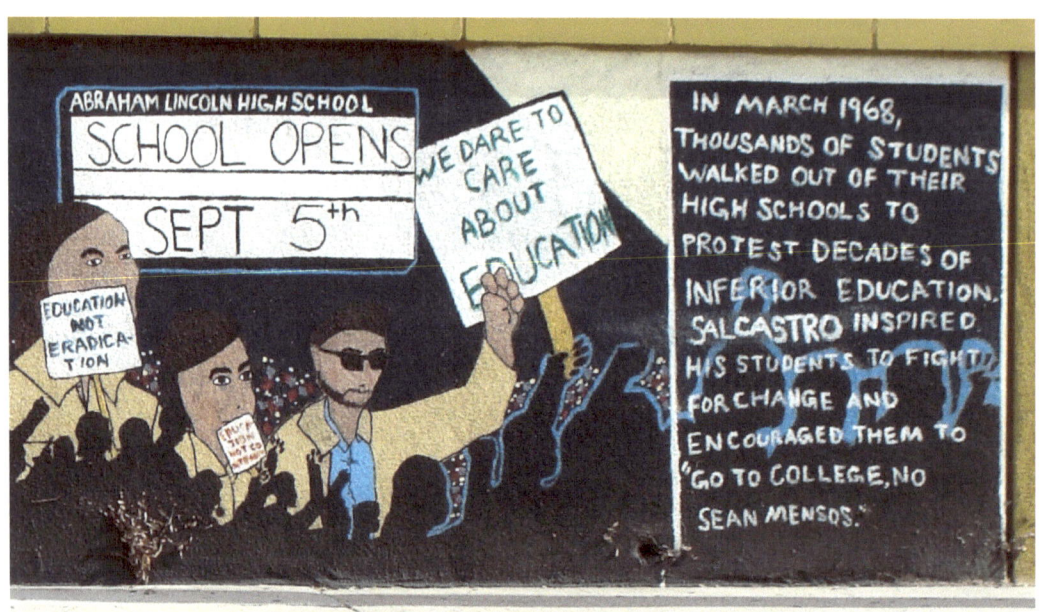

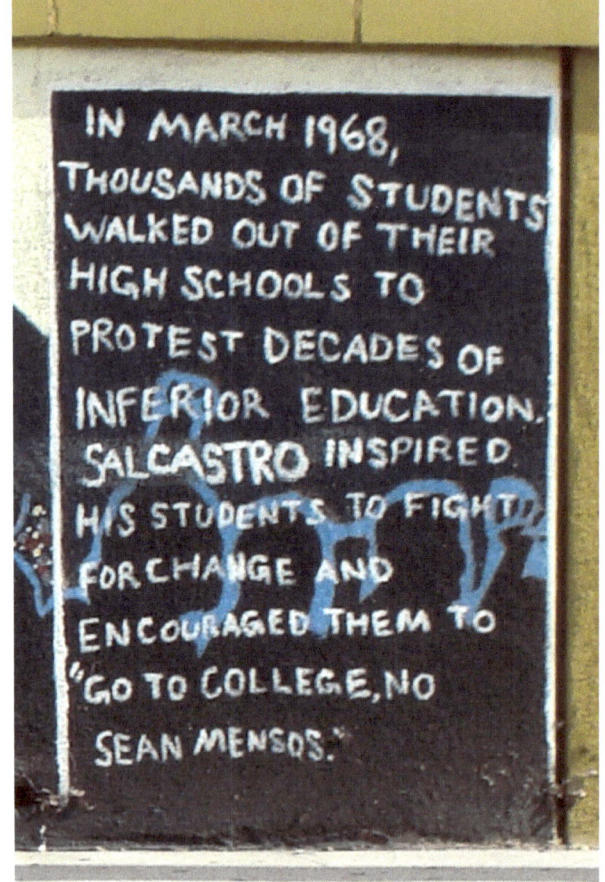

Lincoln High School

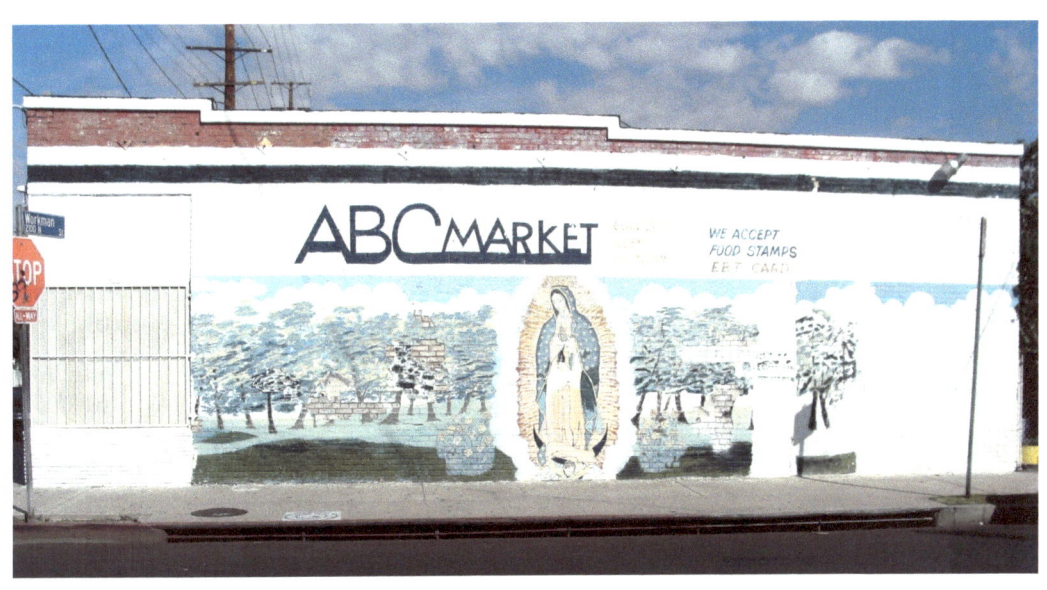

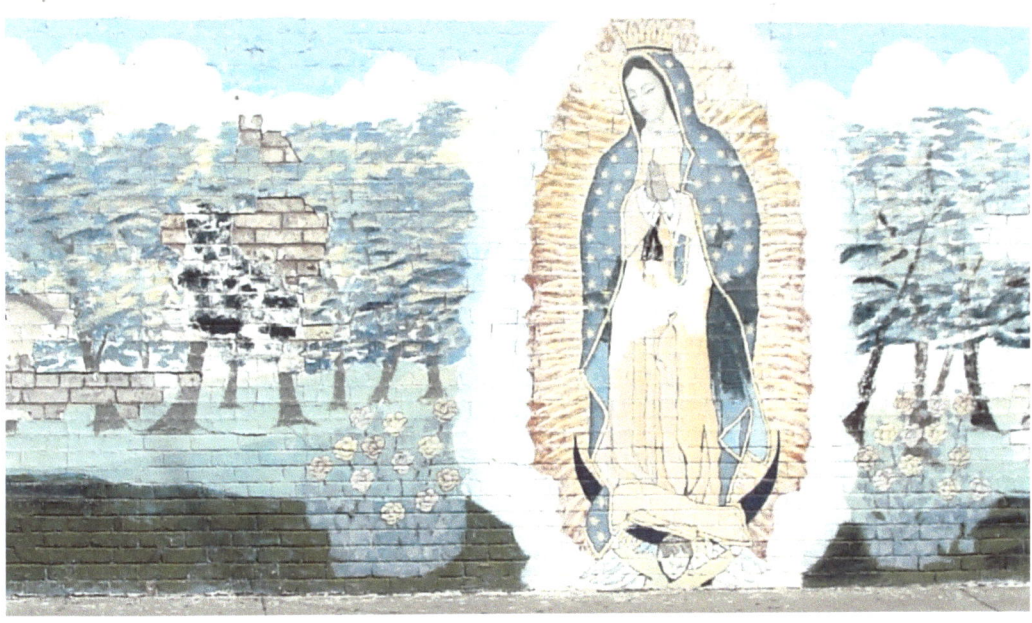

Mozart and Workman

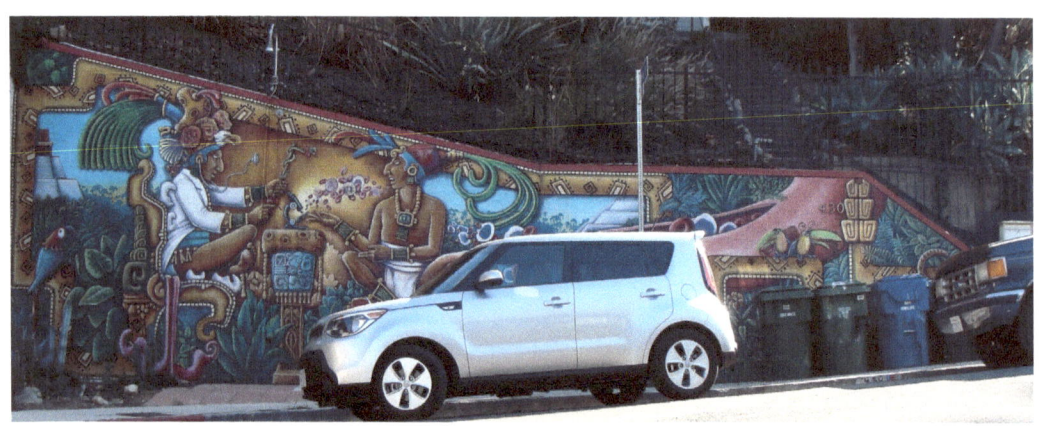

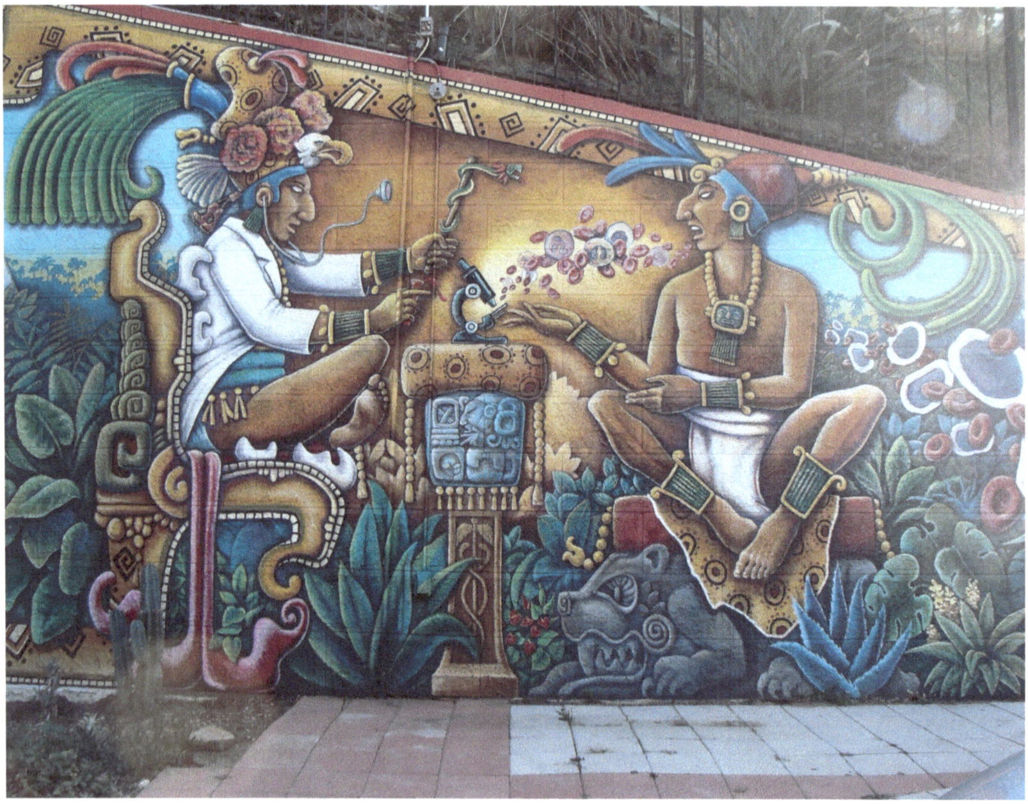

Street north of N Broadway

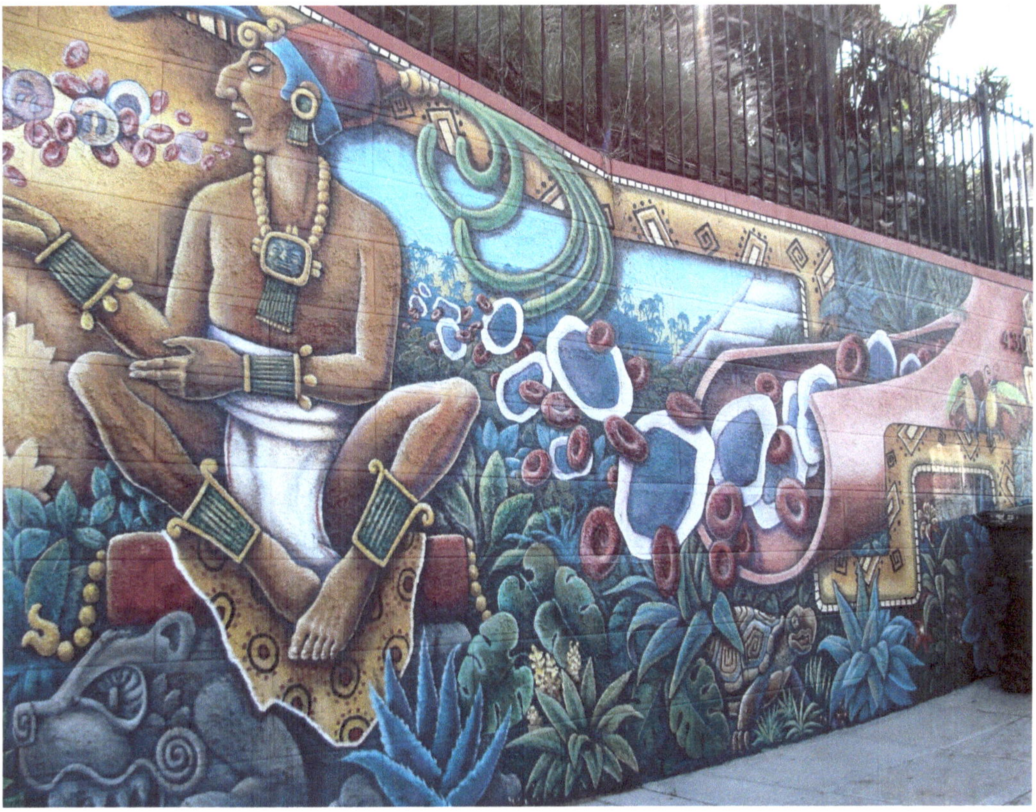

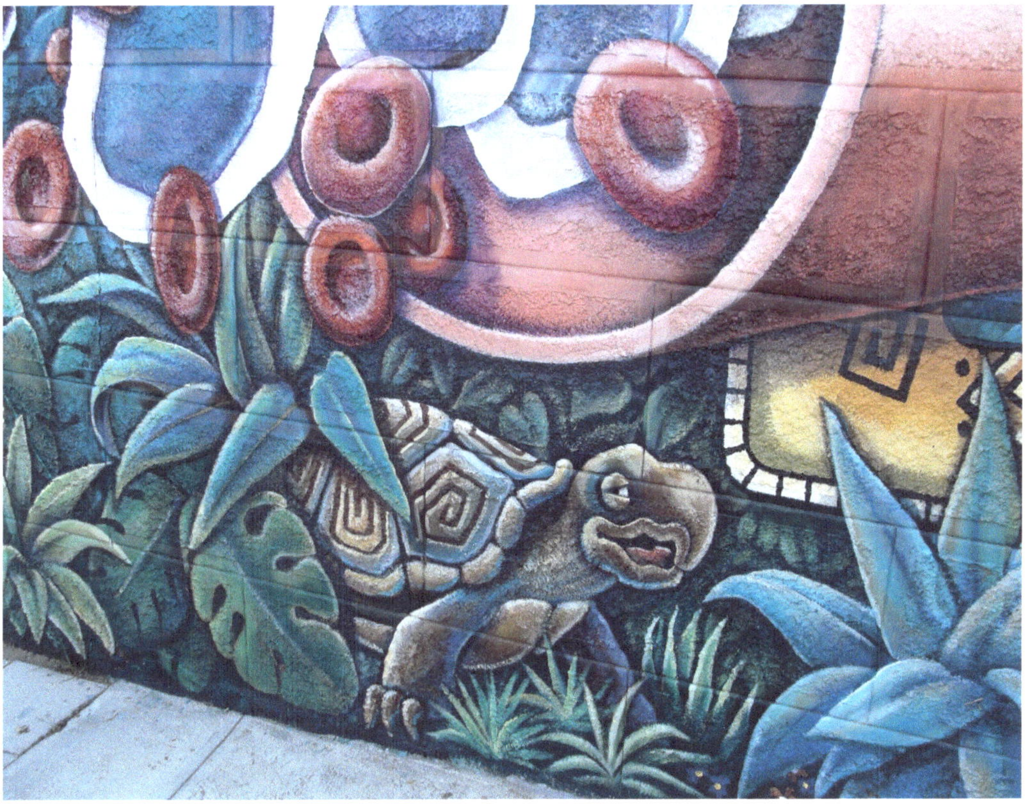

Street north of N Broadway

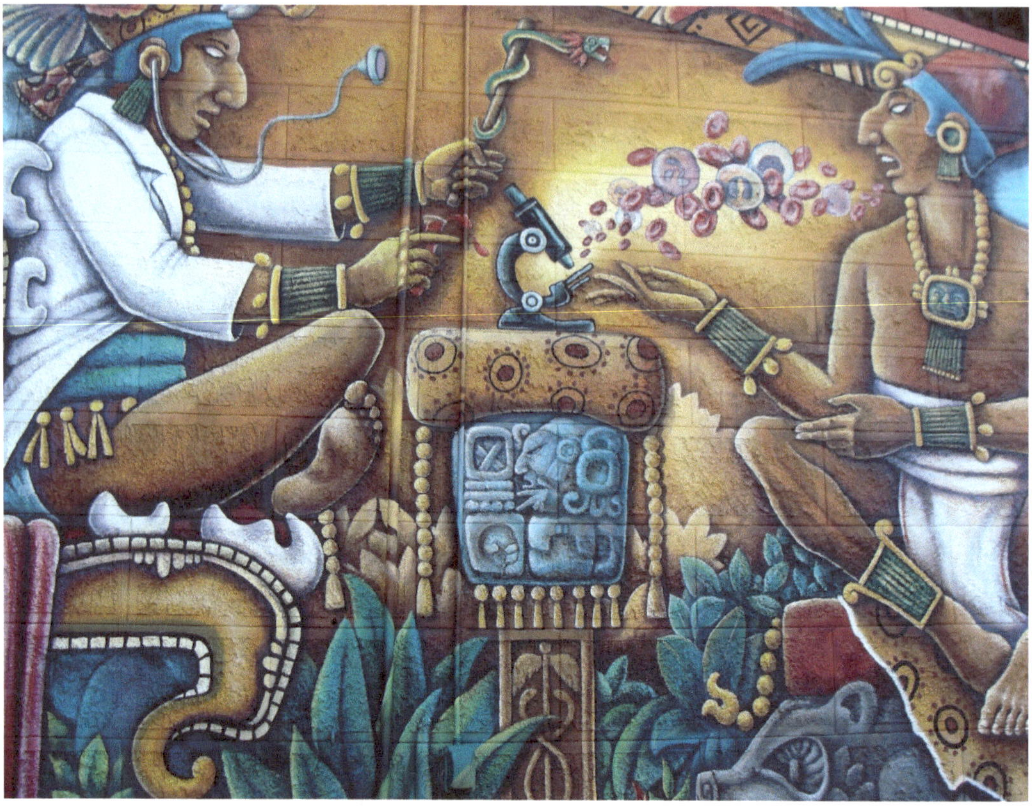

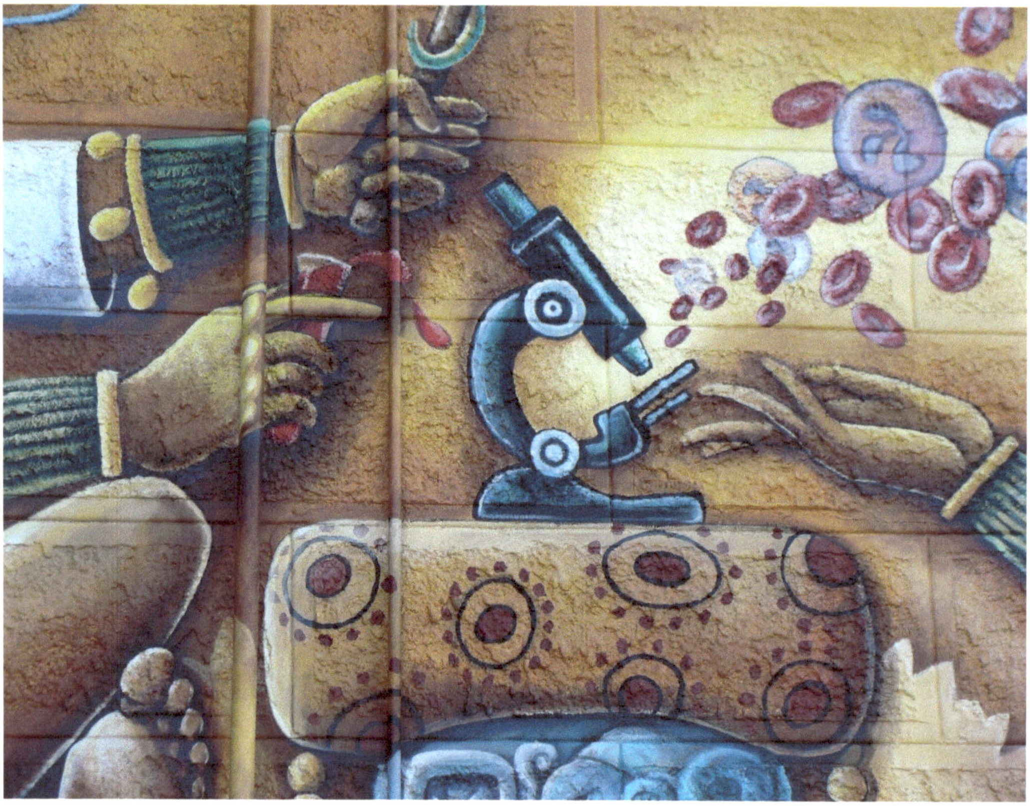

Street north of N Broadway

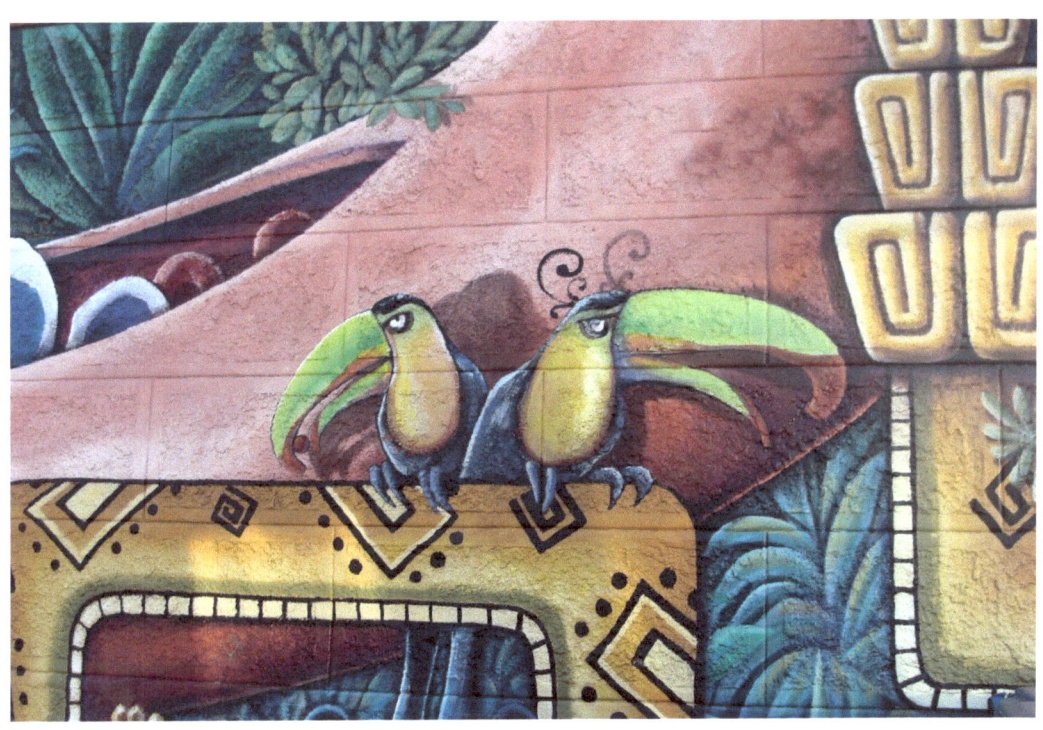

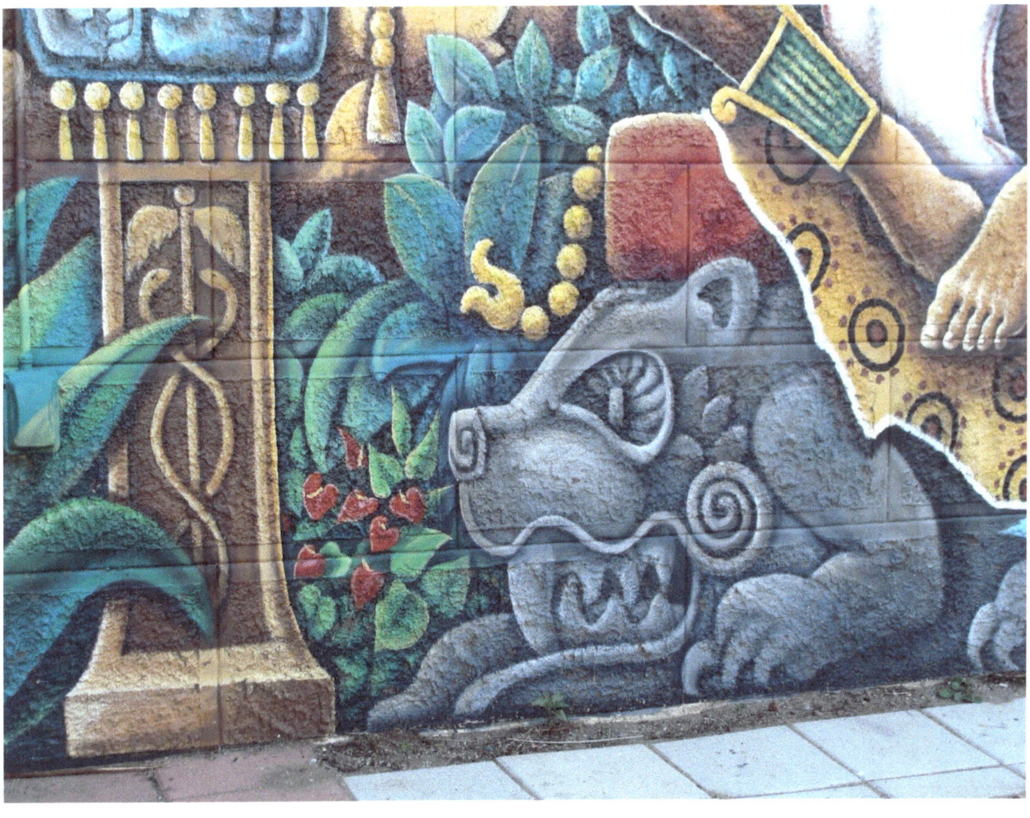

Street north of N Broadway

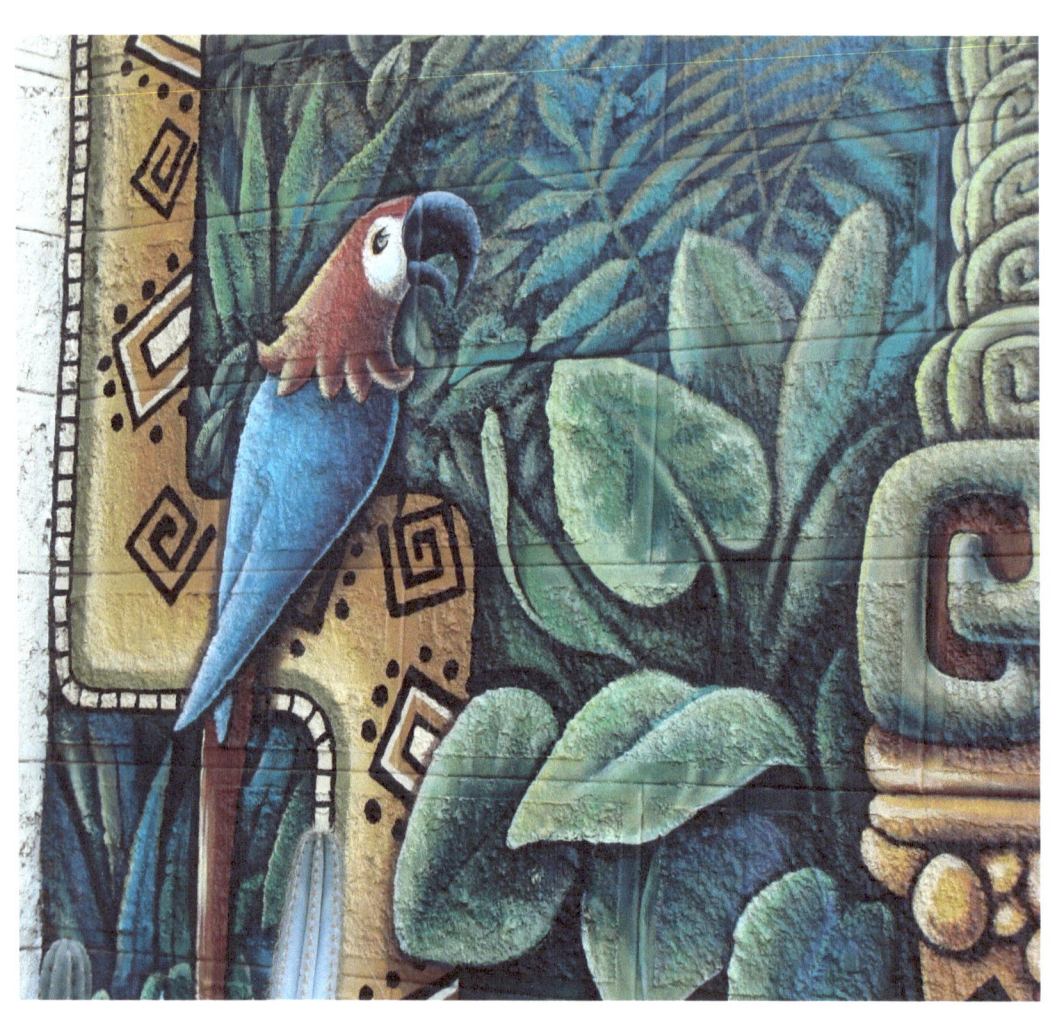

Street north of N Broadway